Ford

Heavy-Duty Trucks

1948 - 1998
Photo History

Paul G. McLaughlin

Iconografix
Photo History Series

Iconografix
PO Box 446
Hudson, Wisconsin 54016 USA

Library of Congress Card Number: 00-135944

ISBN 1-58388-043-7

01 02 03 04 05 06 07 5 4 3 2 1

Printed in the United States of America

Cover and book design by Shawn Glidden

Copyedited by Dylan Frautschi

Cover Caption: 1952 Ford F-8 tractor owned and restored by John Schulze of Anoka, Minnesota. *Photo by Paul G. McLaughlin.*

Book Proposals

Iconografix is a publishing company special-izing in books for transportation enthusiasts. We publish in a number of different areas, including Automobiles, Auto Racing, Buses, Construction Equipment, Emergency Equip-ment, Farming Equipment, Railroads & Trucks. The Iconografix imprint is constantly growing and expanding into new subject areas.

Authors, editors, and knowledgeable enthusi-asts in the field of transportation history are invited to contact the Editorial Department at Iconografix, Inc., PO Box 446, Hudson, WI 54016.

TABLE OF CONTENTS

DEDICATION

It was a warm afternoon in August of 1968 and he was driving back to the dealership where he worked. He had just come from a meeting with a customer where they had discussed the final delivery details on a large fleet of Ford trucks he had sold. Just then he heard a blast from an air horn and one of those trucks passed him by like he was standing still. When he got back to the dealership he went looking for the young man who was driving the truck and read him the riot act about driving these big trucks like sports cars.

You don't have to worry anymore dad because I learned that lesson very well. I don't drive those big Fords like sports cars and I haven't in quite awhile. Rest in peace.

Paul G. McLaughlin
Albuquerque, NM
November 2000

ACKNOWLEDGMENTS

Writing a book of this nature requires help from other individuals who are familiar with the subject and I would like to take this opportunity to thank them for their assistance. Without their help I might not have been able to finish this project.

Don Bunn, Bloomington, MN
Ken Campbell, Albuquerque, NM
Dick Copello, York, PA
Bill Wasner, St. Joseph, MN
Carl King, Everett, MA
Eddie Corbin, Albuquerque, NM
Paul McLaughlin Sr., Arlington, MA
John Schulze, Anoka, MN
Larry Jones, Tijeras, NM
Robert Lucero DDS, Albuquerque, NM
Dennis Maag, St. Louis, MO

Archie Stutt, Hamilton, New Zealand
John McLaughlin, Arlington, MA
John Dupuis, Wisconsin Rapids, WI
Gordon LeFebvre, Elk River, MN
Myron Felix, Cold Spring, MN
David Thompson, Cameron, WI
Elroy Lund Jr, Exeland, WI
Bernice McLaughlin, Albuquerque, NM
Guy Appleman, Albuquerque, NM
Amy McLaughlin, Albuquerque, NM
Jessica McLaughlin, Albuquerque, NM
Paul C. McLaughlin, Albuquerque, NM
Dylan Frautschi, Iconografix, Inc.
Mike Gonzales, Albuquerque, NM
George Hinds, Cambridge, MA

Photographs, unless otherwise noted, were taken by the author.

INTRODUCTION

My fascination with heavy-duty Ford trucks began a long time ago when I was a young boy living in Somerville, Massachusetts. Our family lived on the top floor of an apartment house and this apartment had a lot of windows. A lot of windows where I spent a lot of time checking out the world passing by.

One of those windows looked down on a construction equipment storage yard that was full of "Bonus Built" Ford trucks. I spent a lot of time sitting at that window watching those Fords come and go, and promising myself that one day I would own and drive one of those Ford trucks.

Later on, when my dad began selling Ford trucks and cars, my appreciation for Ford trucks grew even more. Especially when my dad would take me on trips with him in his trucks, or when he would take us by the Somerville Ford Assembly Plant where I saw all sorts of heavy-duty Ford trucks hauling away new cars and trucks.

These experiences so captivated me that I envisioned some day I would own a whole fleet of Ford trucks with an example of every noteworthy Ford truck produced over the last fifty years included–a fleet that would number between 50 and 100 units. The only reason this dream hasn't become a reality yet is that I don't have enough money to buy and maintain a fleet of this size. Nor do I have enough room to store all these trucks properly. However, this dream still lives and who knows what changes the future might bring.

Ford Trucks Forever!
Paul G. McLaughlin

Early 1948 Ford F-8 prototype with box-type van body seen here on a set of truck scales. *Ford Motor Company Photo*

1948-1952
A Time Known as the "Bonus Built" Era

1948

The year of 1948 was a milestone year for the Ford Motor Company and its truck division. Their trucks had an all new look to them, a new series designation for their truck lineup, and for the first time in their history some extra heavy-duty models.

These new Ford trucks made their debut on January 16, 1948. For the first time Ford trucks had a distinct designation which Ford called their "F Series." This new series consisted of eight different model designations ranging from a light-duty, 1/2-ton rated, F-1 pickup all the way up to and including an extra heavy-duty, 3-ton rated, F-8 truck.

Prior to 1948 the heaviest-duty Ford trucks were rated between 1 1/2 and 2 tons, but adding some heavier-duty rated trucks offered Ford a chance to really expand their truck lineup to meet a growing demand for bigger trucks to handle bigger jobs and higher payloads. This book covers heavy-duty models and Ford's entry into this market segment was their F-5 trucks. These trucks, like all Ford heavies of that time, were offered in two cab configurations. A straight conventional cab with a long hood and a shorter cab-over-engine (COE) version, which allowed for a shorter truck that was easier to maneuver in cities and towns or for applications that restricted truck length. In this latter form a longer body or trailer could be used to provide for more cargo capacity and bigger payloads.

The F Series trucks featured new cabs with one-piece windshields and vent windows in their doors. These trucks also had new hoods, new front fenders, and a new grille. There were also changes made inside these new cabs to accommodate more comfortable seating. Another feature found on the exterior of these trucks was Ford's use of more bright-plated trim pieces that really brightened up their looks compared to previous Ford trucks.

A lineup of early 1948-1952 Ford cab-over-engine (COE) trucks await their turn for restoration. Now they sit in a Minnesota farm field just waiting for their time to come.

Once again Ford offered their F-1 through F-6 truck customers the choice of two L head (Flathead) engines. One was an in-line six cylinder that displaced 226 cubic inches and put out a 95 horsepower rating at 3300 rpm. The other engine, also an L head (Flathead) V-8, displaced 239 cubic inches and carried a horsepower rating of 100 at 3800 rpm. The six cylinder was a carry-over engine from the previous year but the V-8, called the "Rouge 239," featured a new block, new cylinder heads, new valves and valve guides, a new crankshaft, new bearings, and a vacuum-controlled distributor.

That new engine was big news, but it wasn't the biggest news to come out of Ford's truck group in 1948. No, the biggest news involved two new extra heavy-duty truck lines for Ford. Ford called them "Big Jobs" and it was easy to see why. These "Big Jobs" were big trucks, the biggest that Ford had ever built, and they rated them at 2 1/2 and 3 tons respectively. The lighter truck was given the F-7 designation while the larger of the two was called the F-8. These two new lines of extra heavy-duty trucks featured longer wheelbases, wider front ends, bigger front fenders, bigger engines, larger clutches and transmissions, bigger brakes, heavier springs, eight stud wheels, and other heavy-duty pieces.

Wheelbases for these brutes were available in lengths of 135, 147, 159, 178, and 195 inches. The F-7 carried a GVW (Gross Vehicle Weight) rating of 19,000 lbs and a cargo rating of 2 1/2 tons. The F-8 trucks carried a GVW of 21,500 lbs with a 3-ton cargo rating. As a straight truck the F-7 models carried a GCW (Gross Combined Weight) of 25,000 lbs, while the F-8 as a straight truck would have a GCW of around 28,000 lbs. However, the maximum GTW (Gross Tractor Weight) when used as a

Myron Felix liked Ford's 1948 truck promotions so much he had one replicated on a signboard that he mounted on the body of his restored 1948 F-6 COE stake bodied truck.

tractor trailer combo was 35,000 lbs for an F-7 and 37,000-39,000 lbs for an F-8. In Canada some of these trucks were rated even higher.

Being that these F-7 and F-8 trucks were rated so high, Ford didn't think that their regular engine offerings would have enough power to get the job done so they specified a new, larger powerplant for these behemoths. Ford called this new engine their "Cargo King V-8" and it was based on Ford's new Lincoln car V-8. It displaced 337 cubic inches and was rated at 145 horsepower at 3600 rpm. This rating was a good one but this engine's strong point was its torque rating of 255 lbs/ft at 1800 rpm—lots of pulling power at a relatively low engine speed. It was just what a heavy-duty truck needed back in 1948.

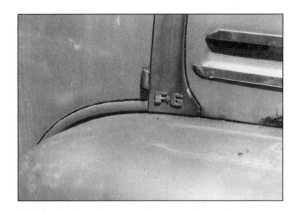

Top photo. On early model Ford COE's, Ford mounted the series designation trim piece between the hood opening and the door, just above the front fenders.

Middle photo. This photo shows the side trim details on 1948 Ford COE trucks.

Bottom photo. A 1948/1949 Ford heavy-duty truck hauls a crane these days. Note that the top of the cab has been cut away on one side to facilitate carrying the boom when it is in the down position.

There are still a lot of old Ford trucks sitting undiscovered in yards and fields around the USA. This diamond-in-the-rough Ford "gem" sits in a storage yard in Southern Colorado.

1949

The year of 1949 saw more of the same for Ford's heavy-duty and extra heavy-duty trucks, but let us take a few minutes to discuss these trucks in detail. Ford promoted these trucks as "Built Stronger To Last Longer," which might explain why so many of them are still seen today over fifty years after the last one was built.

Once again Ford's heavy-duty lineup started out with the F-5 trucks in either conventional or cab-over-engine styles. Ford claimed at that time that this truck outsold all its competition in this market segment. Whether this claim was true or not, we'll probably never know today.

The F-5 trucks for this year carried a GVW of 14,000 lbs and were available with either a single-speed or a two-speed rear end. The transmission used was a four-speed manual with ratios of 6.40:1 (1st gear), 3.09:1 (2nd gear), 1.69:1 (3rd gear), 1.00:1 (4th gear), and a 7.83:1 (reverse).

Below. In this shot we can see all the details that distinguish the front ends of 1948-1950 Ford F Series COE trucks.

Up next on the 1949 heavy-duty F Series roster was the F-6 truck line with a GVW rating of 15,500 lbs. Features found on this truck included the choice of either the "Rouge 226" six-cylinder engine or the "Rouge 239" V-8. Again the horsepower ratings were 95 for the former and 100 for the latter. Other features included a double channel frame, removable brake drums, needle bearing steering, and something called a "level action suspension system." One also had his or her choice of different wheelbases to cover a wide range of bodies including some factory catalogued bodies.

Next on the agenda was the lightest of the "Big Jobs," the F-7, which carried a GVW rating of 19,000 lbs. Power for this truck was again the "Rouge 337 V-8" and was still rated at 145 horsepower. Other features found on this truck included a "Million Dollar Cab," 5-speed manual transmission with overdrive or direct drive in 5th gear, a double channel frame, and large, power-assisted brakes.

Finally, the "Extra Heavy-duty Champion" for this year was the F-8 "Big Job." Like in 1948, this series of trucks carried a GVW rating of 21,500 lbs. It was equipped with everything the F-7 had plus heavier-duty springs, shocks, brakes, rear axles, etc.

Colors offered on the 1949 models were Vermillion (red), Meadow Green, Medium Luster Black, Birch Gray, and a Chrome Yellow. They also offered Fleet Colors for buyers who bought more than one or two trucks.

Above. A heavy-duty Ford truck believed to be a 1949 model works out at a lumberyard back then. Though it can't be seen in this photo, there is a Marmon-Herrington emblem on the side of its hood indicating that it has been modified with a Marmon-Herrington All-Wheel Drive System. *Bill Fox Collection*

Photo at right. In order to gain easier access into the COE cab Ford provided an auxiliary step/cover for one to step up onto.

1950

The "Bonus Built" Ford trucks were entering their third model year in 1950 and to keep buyer's interested in their truck products Ford made some changes across the board to make all their models look fresher.

Ford offered some new models in the F-3 line for this year, which helped to expand Ford's truck lineup to some 175 different models. Like before, these trucks were offered with either a 226-cubic-inch six-cylinder or a 239-cubic-inch V-8 engine. Looking at the six cylinder, it was offered in everything from the F-1 through F-6 line of trucks but if that six wasn't powerful enough to get the job done and the customer didn't want a V-8, Ford had a new engine ready to go that was made available to F-6 buyers. This engine came from Ford's Transit Bus program and it was called either the "Big Six" or

the "Rouge 254." This 254-cubic-inch L head in-line six-cylinder engine put out a rated 110 horsepower at 3400 rpm and its torque rating was even better at 212 lbs/ft at 1200 rpm. Those ratings were higher than the "Rouge 239 V-8" and in some cases the more powerful six-cylinder engine had better fuel economy numbers, which was a strong selling point back in 1950.

If you preferred the V-8, the "Rouge 239" was still the engine of choice in the F-1 through F-6 line of trucks and the "Rouge 337" still powered the F-7 and F-8 "Big Jobs."

The "Big Six" wasn't the only big news at the Ford truck works in 1950. The big news with F-7 trucks for this year was the fact that they were available with larger hydraulic rear brakes, while the larger F-8 could now be had with full air brakes. A longer, 176-inch wheelbase chas-

This complete 1949 Ford F-8 truck sits in a storage yard. Other than weathering of its paint and worn tires it looks to be in pretty good condition.

Ford Cab-Over-Engine trucks when fixed up make for some neat-looking hauling vehicles as shown in this photo taken at a car show a few years ago.

Red seems to have been a popular color on Ford trucks in the late 1940s judging by how many old Ford trucks we see with faded red paint.

sis could now be ordered for F-5 and F-6 trucks and the F-7 and F-8 trucks could now be ordered with two new wheelbases of 147 and 178 inches, on top of the regular wheelbase lengths that were offered previously. If you ordered the "Big Six" it came with an extra heavy-duty clutch and a "Synchro-Silent" 4-speed transmission. The "Big Job" trucks got a revised double channel frame and new single-speed rear axles. Finally the F-6's maximum GVW rating was raised to 16,000 lbs with a maximum GCW of 28,000 lbs when used as a tractor trailer rig.

Ford's F Series trucks were starting to look a little dated towards the end of the 1950 model year and Ford knew that in order to compete successfully in the truck market of that time, they had to make some major changes or they would surely lose market share—something they could ill afford to do. It was back to their drawing boards to make the F Series trucks look really new.

Gordy LeFebvre, of Elk River, Minnesota, restored this beautiful 1950 Ford stake bodied truck to better than new condition.

Old Ford fire trucks seem to be popular today and you see a number of them at truck shows these days. Most of them seem to be 1950 models as the one shown here.

John Dupuis, of Wisconsin Rapids, Wisconsin, has restored this 1950 Ford F-8 tractor, which sports an original "Deluxe Ford Sleeper Cab" by Orrville Body Company of Orrville, Ohio. *John Dupuis Photo*

1951

Starting at the front, the new 1951 Fords featured a new grille that was comprised of one horizontal bar that was supported by three vertical posts and three round-looking orbs. This grille replaced the plain flat horizontal bar motif previously used on the 1948-1950 models. In order to make this grille change Ford had to modify the grille cavity and lower front fender areas.

Moving up from the grille area Ford made some changes in their F Series hood design and trim pieces that helped to readily distinguish the new 1951 hood from the 1950 units they replaced. Another change, a major one, involved the rear of the cab, which now sported a wider and larger rear window that really improved visibility towards the back of the truck.

Ford promoted these redesigned cabs as their "Five Star Cab" in 1951. The "Five Star Cabs" were good-looking cabs in their own right but Ford figured there might be some buyers who wanted something extra in the way of a deluxe cab, so this year they offered

both. They offered the standard "Five Star Cab" and a deluxe version called the "Five Star Extra." The "Five Star Extra," as the name implies, offered the Ford truck buyer in 1951 the opportunity to buy a cab that offered more truck for his money (for a few dollars more, of course). This cab featured extras like a foam rubber pad in the seat covered by a two-tone seat covering, and a perforated thermacoustic headlining material, which covered a glass and wool insulating pad that covered the inside of the roof panel. There was also some extra sound deadening

Another restored Ford fire truck at a truck show seen in Colorado about ten years ago. This one came all the way from Massachusetts.

material placed on the floor, on the doors, and on the inside of the rear cab panel to cut down on noise entering the cab. These "Five Star Extra" cabs were also fitted with deluxe door panels, dual adjustable sun visors, dual armrests, a glove box lock, dual electric horns, and a dome light switch that was controlled by door-mounted switches. In addition to all those "extras" this deluxe version of Ford's F Series truck also came with extra chrome-plated trim on its hood, a chrome-plated windshield band, door locks on both doors, an illuminated cigar lighter, and bright-plated escutcheons on its inside door handles and window cranks. You

Opposite page top. This 1951 Ford dump truck, equipped with a Five-Star Extra Cab, is still working hard almost fifty years after it was built.

Opposite page bottom. The Millstadt Fire Department of Millstadt, Illinois, used this 1951 Ford F-6 COE fire truck well into the 1980s when it was retired from active duty. Today it is used for parades. *Dennis J. Maag Photo*

couldn't find some of this equipment on other trucks, which made the "Five Star Extra" Ford cabs really stand out from the crowd—another strong selling point for these trucks in 1951.

Besides all the changes we have already discussed on the 1951 F Series Ford trucks, Ford's marketing people decided to do a little promoting on the economy aspects of these trucks for this year. They came up with a new promotional campaign revolving around the premise that "Ford Trucking Costs Less," a theme they were more than willing to exploit through a number of promotional tools. One of the best promotional tools they used was to publish a booklet called the "Ford Truck Economy Run" that was distributed to customers at Ford showrooms throughout the year. This 144-page booklet listed the costs associated with running Ford trucks that Ford obtained from surveying about 5,500 previous Ford truck buyers. This book contained the testimonials from Ford truck owners that ran the gamut from the F-1 pickup buyer through to the monster F-8 trucks. It was a good way for Ford to promote their trucks and for customers to use as a guide in ordering a new truck that would be economical to run.

Below. Here is an example of the Five Star Extra "Big Job" trim that Ford used in 1952. Pretty fancy for a truck, huh?

Moving out of the economy sector, a number of improvements were noted on the "Rouge 337 V-8" for this year for both F-7 and F-8 trucks. These improvements included a higher lift camshaft, external coolant bypass tube, new thermostats, a six-blade fan, and a larger radiator.

If you were looking to add options to your 1951 Ford truck the Ford catalogue offered quite a few to choose from. They are listed below. Remember, these were extra cost options and some of these items are pretty hard to find today because they were probably rarely ordered when new.

At the start of the model year 1951 Ford truck grilles were painted an argent silver color but by the end of the model year these grilles were painted an off-white, or ivory color. This was done to cut back the use of some vital materials that were needed for the Korean War effort.

1951 Ford Truck Accessories (optional at extra cost)

120 Amp/Hr Heavy-duty Battery (Standard on F-7, F-8, and School Bus Chassis)
135 Amp/Hr Heavy-duty Battery
Directional Turn Signals
Fire Extinguisher
Locking Gas Cap
40 Amp/Hr Heavy-duty Generator (Standard on F-7 and F-8)
60 Amp/Hr Heavy-duty Generator
Governor (Standard on 254 Six and 337 V-8)
Engine Compartment Light
Road Lamps with Brackets
Spot Light with Bracket (Left Side)
Right Side Stop and Taillight
Utility Lamp
Reflector Flares and Flags
Radiator Grille Guard
Radio (7 Tube with Rectifier and Antenna)
Long Arm Adjustable Exterior Rear View Mirrors
Seat Covers
Starting Crank
Right Hand Sun Visor
Front Tow Hooks
Vacuum Pump for Wipers (V-8)
Vacuum Reserve Tank for Power Brakes
Windshield Washer
Windshield Glare Filter Frame
Side Mount 25-Gallon Fuel Tank
Running Boards
Frame Extensions
Shock Absorbers
Behind Cab Tire Carrier (F-5, F-6)
Rear Frame Tire Carrier (F-7, F-8)

1952

1951 was a hard act to follow for Ford's trucking department, but they were determined to keep the momentum going. The big news at Ford truck for 1952 was the availability of a new, overhead valve six-cylinder engine in some Ford truck models. This new engine was smaller than the 226 L head that it replaced, but it put out more power and was more economical to boot—two appealing properties for truck buyers back then. This new engine displaced some 215 cubic inches and was available on F-1 through F-5 trucks. It put out 101 horsepower compared to the 95 rating the previous engine offered. Ford called this engine their "Cost Clipper 6" probably in deference to the fact it was cheaper to run than the old "Flathead" six that it replaced.

Ford didn't forget their V-8 buyers for this year because they made some changes to the "Rouge 239" to make it a better powerplant. Those changes helped to boost the horsepower rating to 110. This was good news to Ford salesmen who were trying to sell V-8 engines as options in F-1 through F-6 trucks. This was a hard selling job at times when Ford's "Big Six" and "Little Six" put out a higher rating than the V-8.

John Schulze, of Anoka, Minnesota, restored this "Big Job" F-8 tractor to like-new condition. This truck turns heads wherever it goes.

However, the higher horsepower "Rouge 239" wasn't the biggest Ford V-8 news in 1952. No, that honor rested with the new overhead valve V-8 engines that were featured in F-7 and F-8 trucks for this year. The F-7 "Big Job" got a new "Y Block V-8" that displaced some 279 cubic inches. This engine was called Ford's "Cargo King" V-8 and it carried the same horsepower rating of 145 at 3800 rpm that the previous Lincoln-based Flathead V-8 used in 1948-1951 trucks. Its torque rating was now set at 244 lbs/ft at 1900-2100 rpm. This new engine was equipped with hydraulic lifters, five main bearings, a bore of 3.56 inches and a stroke of 3.50 inches. Other features found on this engine were cast rocker arms, and a Holley 2V carburetor.

The F-8 also had a new "Cargo King" V-8 in 1952. The F-8 "Cargo King" V-8 was an overhead valve "Y Block" also, but it displaced some 317 cubic inches. This bigger "Cargo King" V-8 had a horsepower rating of 155 at 3900 rpm and a torque rating of 285 lbs/ft at a low 1700-2000 rpm. Because of these more powerful engines Ford gave their "Big Jobs" higher GVW and GCW ratings.

The 1952 Ford trucks, which Ford promoted as the "World's Greatest Trucks," looked like the 1951 models they replaced except for some minor trim items found on their hoods. Also, 1952 models received a set of block letters that spelled out the word F O R D on their upper grille panels just like what was done on previous 1948-1950 models (an area that had a V-8 emblem, when so equipped, on 1951 versions).

The "Bonus Built" Ford line of F Series trucks had done Ford well for almost five years, but the time had come for Ford to make some dramatic changes to their trucks, and they did so as evidenced by the new Ford trucks that debuted as 1953 models.

Rear three quarter view of John Schulze's 1952 Ford F-8 "Big Job" truck shows that the truck has been equipped with rear fenders, saddle tanks, a "headache rack," and a custom rear panel full of lights and mud flaps.

This 1952 F-6 Ford fire truck from St. Peters, Missouri, is equipped with a Towers 500-gpm pumper body. It is a sharp-looking fire truck with all its period accessories. *Dennis J. Maag Photo*

Specification Sheet 1952 Ford Trucks

Model	Rating	Maximum Payloads
F-5	Heavy-duty	9,570 Pounds
F-6	Heavy-duty	11,305 Pounds
F-7	Extra Heavy-duty	12,865 Pounds
F-8	Extra Heavy-duty	15,465 Pounds
F-5 COE	Heavy-duty	9,350 Pounds
F-6 COE	Heavy-duty	10,445 Pounds
F-5 School Bus	36 Passengers	7,900 Pounds
F-6 School Bus	54 Passengers	10,445 Pounds

F-5: Maximum GVW 14,000 Pounds
Maximum GCW 24,000 Pounds
Wheelbases 134, 158, and 176 inches

F-6: Maximum GVW 16,000 Pounds
Maximum GCW 28,000 Pounds
Wheelbases 134, 158, 176 inches

F-7: Maximum GVW 19,000 Pounds
Maximum GCW 38,000 Pounds
Wheelbases 135, 147, 159, 178, and 195 inches

F-8: Maximum GVW 22,000 Pounds
Maximum GCW 41,000 Pounds
Wheelbases 135, 147, 159, 178, and 195 inches

They don't come much tougher than this 1953 Big Job F-700 truck photographed at one of Ford's test tracks in 1952. Note the new crest on the front of the hood and the V-8 emblem in the grille. *Ford Motor Company Photo*

1953-1956
"Driverized" Cabs and "Fat-fendered" Looks

1953

1953 was a great year to go Ford, be it a car or truck. This was Ford's "Golden Anniversary" year and they pulled out all the stops to celebrate this milestone year with their employees, dealers, and customers.

Ford had redesigned their 1952 car lines, they just cleaned up some trim items to freshen up the look of their cars, but it was a different story altogether as far as their truck models were concerned. In this year, the Ford truck division made wholesale changes to their product line to make it look entirely different from what came before.

Ford called these new trucks their "Economy Trucks," but they pushed that economy aspect only as a secondary function for this year. Their primary focus centered on their redesigned cabs, which they defined as being "driverized," a term that was probably coined in the Ford Design Studio in the early 1950s. Be that as it may, by "driverized," Ford was trying to point out that these cabs were designed with the driver's comfort and convenience in mind. Ford figured, and rightly so, that if a driver was comfortable in these new cabs that their trucks would be easier to sell. Ford even had a promotional campaign going on at that time called their "Fifteen Second Test" whereby they challenged drivers and truck buyers alike to climb into the cab and try it out for fifteen seconds or more. They were pretty confident that once somebody actually sat in this cab and tried it out, either as a driver or passenger, they would appreciate all the time and effort that Ford spent making the interior a more pleasant environment for somebody to work in. This effort went so far that Ford actually used life-size dummies, three of them, to set the parameters needed to reach the results they wanted. From these studies they came up with a wider, more comfortable seat, and the idea to centralize all the controls and gauges in front of the driver so that the effort to operate this truck would be less tiring and stressful. Though

This is what a Ford Custom Cab interior looked like
in 1953. Pretty fancy for a truck, huh? *Ford Motor
Company Photo*

they probably didn't know it at the time, this was probably the first time that ergonomics were used in car and truck design, and in 1953 the science of ergonomics wasn't even thought of yet.

Though what Ford accomplished on the interiors of these trucks was important, let us not forget about all the exterior changes they made on these trucks to make them look entirely different than the "Bonus Built" trucks that preceded them. Besides the redesigned cabs, another redesigned feature was the front fenders, which were designed a lot "fatter" than the earlier trucks. Those fat fenders have made these trucks popular ever since they first turned a wheel on the highways and byways around the world.

These new Fords also used a flatter, wider hood that seemed to flow into those front fenders, creating a more unified look than the hood and fender combination used before. Besides the new hoods and front fenders, these trucks also sported a new grill treatment, which featured a single, wide, horizontal bar that separated two headlight pods. These grilles were painted off-white and had two wide slots that flowed from the headlight pods in towards the center. Trucks equipped with V-8 engines had a V-8 emblem mounted on the center of this grille bar. Six-cylinder trucks had a nondescript three-pointed star-like emblem mounted in the same spot. Deluxe, Custom Cab trucks featured six chrome-plated trim pieces located in the slotted areas of the grille bar. Another new feature found on the front of these trucks was a new Ford truck emblem that was mounted on the front center section of the hood. This new emblem was a crest with the Ford name in block letters embossed on its top with the body of the crest painted red, with a chrome-plated cog gear bisected by a thunderbolt. The emblem was indicative of the power found under the hoods of these new Fords.

The cabs used on these trucks were wider and had more glass area to give the interior a lighter, more airy cab environment. They also used new, wider doors to make ingress and egress easier.

A 1953 Ford COE sits under a tree in its retirement years. It probably wouldn't take too much to make it roadworthy again.

When all was said and done it was easy to see where Ford spent all their money in redoing their F Series trucks. Ford claims it spent some $30 million on this change-over and with all the changes we saw that number was probably pretty close to the actual figure.

There was one other item that should be mentioned about the new 1953 Ford trucks. This item was a major one in that Ford changed the way they designated their F Series trucks for this year. The F-1 was now called the F-100, the F-2 was now the F-250, the F-3 was now called the F-350, and so on and so forth. In addition, the COE (Cab-Over-Engine) models now carried their own designations. They became Ford's "C" Series and were labeled as the C-500, C-600, C-750, and C-800.

Above. Ford debuted a new truck crest shown here, with their new 1953 trucks.

1954

With all the changes we saw with the new 1953 Ford trucks one would think that there couldn't possibly be any changes that Ford could make for their 1954 truck line, but change them they did—and those changes were for the better.

First and foremost was a new line of short stroke, overhead valve, V-8 engines that provided a lot of power potential at a lower cost than the Flathead V-8 engines used before. Ford called these engines either "Power Kings" or "Cargo Kings." The smallest, least powerful "Power King" was a 239-cubic-inch V-8 rated at 130 horsepower at 4200 rpm. The next engine was the "Power King 256," which was a truck modified Mercury engine of the same displacement. This engine was rated at 138 horsepower at 3900 rpm and had a torque rating of 226 lbs/ft at 1900-2400 rpm. Both of these engines, as well as a new 223-cubic-inch "Cost Clipper Six" rated at 115 horsepower, were available in F-600 trucks for this year. The F-600 was Ford's lowest rated heavy-duty model line now.

Moving up the line to the new "Cargo King" V-8s, the first engine was a 279-cubic-inch version that was rated at 152 horsepower at 3800 rpm. It also had a torque rating of 246 lbs/ft at a low of 1800-2400 rpm. This engine, as well as the "Power King 256," was used in the F-700, the T-700, the C-750, and the B-750 School Buses.

The last "Cargo King" V-8, a 317-cubic-inch engine, was reserved for use in the "Big Job" F-800, "Big Job" F-900, T-800, C-800, and C-900 trucks. The engine put out some 170 horsepower at 3900 rpm with a torque rating of 286 lbs/ft at 1700-2300 rpm.

Ford rated all their "Big Job" trucks, F-700 and above, as extra heavy-duty units. The biggest and baddest "Big Job" for this year was the F-900, but this wasn't the only truck they promoted as being tough. Other tough bruiser trucks in the Ford lineup for this year were the C-900, which carried the same GVW (27,000 lbs) and GCW (Max 55,000 lbs) as the F-900. Still, there was a Ford truck for this year that had higher GVW and GCW ratings than either one of those other tough Fords. This new model was called the T-800 and it carried a GVW of 40,000 lbs and a maximum GCW rating of 60,000 lbs. That "T" in the designation stood for "tandem rear axle" model and this "T" truck was the first Ford factory-built model that came out with a tandem rear axle, or "bogey" unit as it is referred to in trucking parlance.

Ford offered two versions of their tandem axle trucks for this year. The lighter version of the two was called the T-700 with the bigger unit being referred to as the T-800. Both trucks featured an Eaton-Hendrickson tandem axle setup. This setup had power routed to a power divider that was mounted on top of the front axle and the power was then distributed to both rear axles. Both axles were supported by dual, equalizing beams mounted under them with torque rods mounted on top of the axle housings, which were run to a reinforced frame member. This full floating arrangement allowed both axles to move independently of each other. Mounting these axles this way also allowed trucks so equipped to carry heavier payloads. Besides their reinforced frames, these trucks were also equipped with stronger axles, bigger brakes, power steering, bigger springs, etc.

After covering major changes like these it seems that covering a grille and trim change would be considered pretty insignificant on the 1954 Fords. However, for the sake of identification, these new Fords carried a redesigned grille that featured a large horizontal bar that looked entirely different from the 1953 version. This large bar was supported by two smaller vertical bars. V-8 powered trucks used a chromed V-8 emblem mounted in the center of this grille bar while six-cylinder trucks featured a chrome-plated stylized four-pointed star. Custom Cab trucks used chrome-plated hash marks, which flanked either ornament. The Ford truck crest was still used in the front center of the hood.

Opposite page bottom. This 1954 Ford "Big Job" fire engine belongs to the Festus Fire Department of Festus, Missouri. It has been fitted with a 750-gpm Howe Pump Body. *Dennis J. Maag Photo*

This "Big Job" F-700 Ford truck was found in a
Colorado truck yard about five years ago. It sits in
this yard with a bunch of other old Ford trucks.

1955

There weren't many changes to report on the 1955 models from Ford. Ford still promoted their short-stroke V-8 engines and they called these trucks their "Money Makers." Once again Ford changed the grille on the 1955 models and this time the design looked like they used two separate horizontal grille bars. The bottom bar was straight, however the upper bar featured a "v" drop in its center that dropped down to touch the lower bar. V-8 and six-cylinder trucks once again used separate ornamentation, which was located in the "v" area of the upper bar. The 1955 models also used different side trim on their hoods.

In spite of the fact that Chevrolet, Ford's chief rival in the trucking business, introduced a redesigned truck halfway through the model year, Ford still managed to increase their market share in 1955. The year 1955 would prove to be the best Ford truck year as far as sales were concerned since the late-1920s.

A little bodywork and paint can make this 1955 Ford COE look good again. The extra trim on the grille bar, the roof drip bar, and upper door identify it as a Custom Cab model.

For 1955 Ford changed the grille design into a two-bar type setup with a "v bar" atop a straight bar arrangement. The V-8 emblem indicates that this truck has one of Ford's "Y Block" V-8 engines.

A 1955 Ford COE "C" model tractor pulls a tanker trailer in an industrial setting in Michigan back in 1954. *Ford Motor Company Photo*

1956

With all the changes that the competition made to their trucks in 1955, Ford knew they had to make some changes to their 1956 models or lose out on market share and be left behind. Though they would have liked to debut a new looking truck in 1956, that wouldn't be possible, so they had to make do with what they had on hand. They instructed their designers and engineers to go back to their drawing boards and try to freshen up the current body to make it last a little longer. This was no easy task but the designers and engineers accepted the challenge and proceeded to work on this interim model that would keep them in the ball game for 1956. The end result of their hard work was a truck that shared the body, cabs, fenders, and hood of the 1953-1955 models but looked quite a bit different than them. In one quick stroke Ford had managed to pull a rabbit out of the hat, a rabbit that literally saved their skin.

What those designers did was to alter the upper cab, cowl, windshield posts, and top panel to accept a curved, wraparound windshield that totally changed the look of these Fords. Besides the areas that we already mentioned, Ford had to alter the doors as well to make the unit work as a whole.

It probably cost Ford millions of dollars to make these changes but that was money well spent, because though they bore some resemblance to earlier models, these trucks appealed to a wide segment of the truck market at that time and Ford sold a lot of them.

The changes that Ford made on their 1956 trucks that were already mentioned were good, but they weren't the only changes that Ford made to make these trucks more appealing. Changes like converting the electrical system over to 12 volts to make the trucks easier to start, or the fact that you could now get your Ford truck with tubeless tires. Ford also made a number of safety related changes for this year

A new load of 1956 Ford trucks sit on a new car hauler trailer that is being pulled by a 1955 Ford COE tractor in this promotional photograph. *Dick Copello Collection*

like adding a deep dish steering wheel to cut down on chest injuries resulting from crashes, and adding stronger lock latches on the doors to keep them from opening in the event of an accident. Also, if you wanted them and were willing to pay extra for them, Ford offered safety belts for this year in all their trucks and cars, the first time this type of safety device was used in an American-built car or truck.

Ford didn't stop here with their changes on their 1956 models, not by a long shot. A lot of changes were made that weren't necessarily seen by a cursory look. A lot of changes were made under the hood and involved Ford truck engines. Changes like sodium filled exhaust valve stems to cut down on heat buildup, stress relieved cylinder heads, and higher compression ratios meant to produce more power. There were also enlarged intake passages and new, 18-mm spark plugs—or how about a balanced crankshaft along with aluminum pistons to cut down on reciprocating weight. Some engines came with four-barrel carburetors and hood scoops for better breathing and more power.

Speaking of more power, Ford had a nice new crop of "Y Block" V-8 engines for this year. Leading the lineup of short stroke engines was a new 272-cubic-inch "Power King" V-8 that in various guises put out 158, 167, and 168 horsepower ratings. If these engines were not powerful enough for your needs, Ford could move you up to a new 302-cubic-inch "Cargo King" V-8, a V-8 that could put out 175 or 186 horsepower depending on how it was setup. If the "Cargo King" was short on power for your needs Ford could move you into a bigger

Top. A patriotic 1956 Ford F-800 grain truck is looking good in this photo taken at an American Truck Historical Society show in Denver, Colorado, about ten years ago.

Middle. Graham Trucking Ford Big Job tractor sits in a Colorado field in the early 1990s. Evidently, Graham Trucking liked Ford trucks because we found a number of them during our truck searches.

Bottom. A restored 1956 Ford "Big Job" C-800 hood emblem. It looks like a work of art, doesn't it?

"Torque King" V-8. These brutes displaced 332 cubic inches and carried horsepower ratings of 190 and 200 respectively. Torque ratings were also up on these engines with the lighter version putting out 306 lbs/ft at 2000-2600 rpm with the hopped-up version putting out 316 lbs/ft at 2100-2700 rpm.

Other changes noted on the 1956 Ford trucks included a new grille, new trim, and a new instrument cluster. In Standard Cab form the new 1956 Ford truck grille was painted an off-white color, but the Custom Cab version was treated to a chrome-plated grille. This grille was so popular that Ford sold it as an option for Standard trucks and quite a few buyers opted for this chrome-plated grille, which is probably why we see so many around today.

Another option that was popular on the 1956 models was the "Big Back Window Option" that wrapped the back window around the back of the cab. It mimicked the wraparound windshield, which made it look so right on these trucks. That big back window also made seeing through the back of the truck a lot easier than seeing through the regular back window.

At the beginning of this era of Ford trucks some wondered if these "Economy Trucks" would be able to top what the "Bonus Built" trucks accomplished before them. If anybody at Ford worried about the legacy these trucks would leave behind they shouldn't have. These Fords were very popular at the time and still are today. You can't ask for a better testimonial than that.

Top. Bill Wasner, of Saint Joseph, Minnesota, has restored a number of old Ford trucks over the years including this great-looking 1956 Custom Cab tractor.

Middle. Rear view of Bill Wasner's 1956 F Series tractor. This truck looks as sharp from the rear as it does from the front.

Bottom. A 1956 Ford Custom Cab C Series box van sits in an alley in Albuquerque, New Mexico. At one time it hauled Denver Post newspapers to Albuquerque customers.

Interior shot of a 1956 Ford Custom Cab truck. The two-tone red and gray color combination gives this cab a deluxe appearance.

This prototype 1956 Ford "Big Job" stake body truck was photographed at a construction site. *Ford Motor Company Photo*

Millstadt Rural Fire Protection District of Millstadt, Illinois, owns this 1956 Ford Big Job fire truck. It has been equipped with a Towers 500-gpm pump body. It was in service for more than 30 years. *Dennis J. Maag Photo*

A 1956 Ford F Series tractor pulls a load of new 1958 Ford pickups in this promotional photograph. *Dick Copello Collection*

Myron Felix has been a Ford man for a long time and he has a fleet of Ford trucks, restored and unrestored alike, at his place up in Minnesota.

33

A Big Job 1957 F Series Ford truck sits alongside the used truck lot at Center Ford in Center, Colorado, in April 2000.

1957-1960
A New Look for Fords

1957

With competition being what it was in the mid-1950s, Ford felt they had to make a dramatic change in the way their trucks looked to make them look up-to-date in order to retain their market position. Make such a change they did, because compared to what Ford offered before, the 1957 trucks looked altogether different. Whereas the previous models featured designs that were more rounded in scope, the new Fords had a slab-sided look to them. The new truck cabs were longer and wider and their hoods were a lot wider and flatter to boot. Also, while the 1953-1956 models featured separate "fat" front fenders, the new Ford trucks, especially the light and medium-duty models, had front fenders that were integral with the hood and cab sides. In essence there was just a hint of front fenders on these models. The heavy-duty models, however, had wider front fenders that stuck out from the cab, but these fenders had a flatter, more square look to them than the fenders that were used on earlier models.

Besides the changes that were done on the F Series conventional trucks for 1957, Ford also introduced a new line of "C" Series trucks that Ford called their "Tilt Cabs." For the first time in Ford truck history their cab-over-engine models used a different, unique cab that wasn't shared by other Ford trucks. The beauty of this cab was that it actually tilted forward to expose the engine compartment, chassis, and mechanical component systems to facilitate easier maintenance. This decreased downtime, which was important to truck owners and drivers who made their livings from their trucks being on the road and not in the shop.

This cab was designed and engineered by Ford, but the cab itself was actually built for Ford by the Budd Corporation. Later, this same cab was also used by Mack and other truck manufacturers.

These new Tilt Cabs sported flat front ends and large expanses of glass, especially in the windshield area. They also contained a wide, comfortable three-man seat in their interiors, which made them popular with drivers and trucking companies alike. With all their glass and that wide seat, the end result was that these Tilt Cabs soon got a reputation for having cabs that were bright, airy, roomy, and more comfortable than many of the cabs that were on the market at that time.

Another feature that Ford promoted on these new Tilt Cab trucks was their relatively short BBC (Bumper to Back of Cab) dimension of 82.5 inches. This short treatment allowed for longer bodies, or trailers could be used with these cabs allowing for bigger payloads. The Tilt Cabs were also perfect for states that limited body or trailer lengths. Another plus for the Tilt Cab driver was the fact that he sat closer to the front of

the truck, compared to a conventional truck, which made his truck easier to maneuver in most situations.

All Ford's trucks for 1957 were offered in Standard or Custom Cab forms. The Custom Cab, like before, was a deluxe upgrade, which really made the trucks look special. These trucks had fancier-looking interiors, dual padded sun visors, dual arm rests, locks on both doors, a cigarette lighter, a locking glove-box door, a white steering wheel, a foam-padded seat with a two-tone seat cover, a chrome-plated grille and windshield band, a "Custom Cab" door-mounted plate, and other goodies. All were for a nominal price. These trucks looked especially nice when ordered with a two-tone exterior paint scheme.

Another first for 1957 Ford heavy-duty trucks was the availability of an automatic transmission for those buyers who were tired of shifting manual transmissions. Allison supplied this 6-speed automatic to Ford and Ford called it their "Transmatic" transmission.

Top. This Big Job 1957 F Series Ford truck was converted into a service truck for a Colorado trucking company in the early 1990s.

Middle. A 1957 Ford C Series tractor pulls a trailer full of new 1959 models. When this photo was taken it looks like this truck had been through some pretty rough weather. *Dick Copello Collection*

Bottom. The Herculaneum Volunteer Fire Department of Herculaneum, Missouri, bought this new Ford fire truck in 1957. It was in active service with the department until the late 1990s when it was retired. *Dennis J. Maag Photo*

1958

Though Ford made a big splash in the truck market for 1957, they weren't about to rest on their laurels and let their competition catch up. For 1958, Ford made some major, as well as minor, changes to their truck model lineup.

Let us cover the minor changes first. These changes consisted of some styling upgrades on the exterior as well as in the interiors of these trucks. Looking on the outside front of the truck, notice that Ford has followed the industry standard of going to a dual headlight (per side) system. Those headlights were placed in pods and between those pods Ford installed a new grille for 1958. This grille was made up of a series of horizontal and vertical bars that made the grille look like it was made up of small squares. Ford changed the hood side trim on these models as well. On the inside of these trucks, Ford changed the seat cover treatment and also put anti-sagging springs in their seats

A late 1950s Tilt Cab Ford tractor sits in Bill Wasner's Ford truck parts yard in St. Joseph, Minnesota. It doesn't look like it would require that much effort to fix this truck up.

Below. This sharp looking 1958 Ford F Series fire engine belongs to the Hays, Kansas, Fire Department. It has been fitted with a General Safety 1000-gpm pump body. *Dennis J. Maag Photo*

to make them more comfortable. One other minor change was done to help keep dirt and water out of these cabs. This change was suspended pedals—rather than having pedals that were connected to rods that went through holes in the floor or through the firewall.

As already mentioned, there were some major changes for this year. The biggest change involved new engines that Ford announced in January of 1958. This new series of three engines made up Ford's new "Super-Duty" line. These engines were meant to give Ford's extra heavy-duty trucks a much needed power boost. The smallest of the three, a 401-cubic-inch V-8, put out a rated 226 horsepower with a torque rating of 350 lbs/ft. The middle range engine was a 477-cubic-inch brute that was rated at 260 horsepower with a maximum torque rating of 430 lbs/ft. And lastly, the giant of the trio was a 534-cubic-inch monster that put out a rated 277 horsepower with a whopping 490 lbs/ft of torque on tap. These engines had more than enough power to handle just about any job a trucker would face.

These engines featured electric fuel pumps submerged in their fuel tanks, a three-stage cooling system, an internal oil cooler, wedge-shaped machined combustion chamber, an externally balanced crankshaft, hard faced valves, sodium-filled exhaust valve stems, dual exhausts, a big oil filter, large paper element air filter, 4-barrel carburetor, and a big oil pump mounted on the front of the engine. An alternator was also offered on these engines as an extra cost option.

Along with these new brawnier engines Ford also offered some new extra heavy-duty models for this year to broaden their coverage at the heavier end of the market. Ford had ten of these new models available from an F-850 all the way up to an F-1100 truck. In between these two marks were a C-850, T-850, F-950, C-950, T-950, F-1000, C-1000, and a C-1100, all models carrying higher GVW and GCW ratings.

Other changes of note on the 1958 Ford trucks were electric wipers on V-8 powered trucks and a new 8-speed Road Ranger manual transmission on F-800 and higher-rated trucks that were equipped with air brakes and 7.17:1 rear end gears.

1959

Ford's truck marketing people came up with a new slogan when they introduced their new 1959 lineup. The slogan they came up with was pretty clever in getting their message across with the least amount of words. "Go Fordward for Savings in 1959."

Another Super-Duty 1958-1959 Ford F Series tandem axle truck sits out in a grassy Wisconsin field. It has been fitted with a homemade boom body.

Most of the changes Ford made for 1959 were minor in nature. Once again they changed out the grille and hood side trim. The new grille was simpler in that it just used a series of parallel running horizontal bars. In standard form the grille was painted in an off-white color while the Custom Cab version was chromed. The hood trim change had Ford including a Ford crest in the trim for this year. Light-duty and medium-duty trucks received a new hood design with an air intake-like opening in its front where F O R D block letters were located. Ford's heavy and extra heavy-duty F Series trucks used a carry-over design from 1958. Another change seen on 1959 models was the adoption of a new instrument cluster design on their dashboards.

One Ford truck that hasn't been covered in a while is Ford's School Bus or "B" Series line. For 1959 Ford offered four different school

This beautiful 1959 Ford fire engine was displayed at a truck show in Phoenix, Arizona, in 1998. It is a sharp looking truck and a very good example of what a late 1950s Ford fire truck looked like back then.

Though it doesn't look like much now this 1958-1959 Ford Tilt Cab truck was probably a sharp looking two-tone Custom Cab version when it was new.

buses. There were two medium-duty versions in the B-500 and B-600, as well as two heavy-duty models in the B-700 and B-750 respectively. All the trucks featured Ford's School Bus Safety Chassis and the heavy-duty models featured wheelbases of 245 and 262 inches. Both could carry 66 passengers. The B-700 had a GVW of 21,000 pounds while the B-750 carried a GVW of 22,000 pounds. These school buses used bodies from a number of manufacturers including Superior Coach, Carpenter Body Works, Blue Bird, and the Wayne Works to mention just a few.

1960

Ford was in a certifying mood in 1960. "Certified Economy" was the theme of Ford's marketing promotional campaign for this model year. Besides certifying them for economy, Ford certified them for durability as well as certifying their reliability. There was an awful lot of certifying going on at Ford back then.

To help certify their economy, Ford de-rated the horsepower ratings on most of their truck engines for this year and they even offered two-barrel carburetors as an option for their 401 and 477 super-duty engines.

Once again Ford changed the design on the hood, hood trim, and grille used on light-duty and medium-duty trucks for this year, but the heavy-duty models used the same hood and grille that was used on the 1959 models.

All Ford trucks in 1960 featured a new Ford truck crest design that was worn on the front of their hoods, and Super-Duty models featured a new "Super-Duty" scripted trim piece that flanked this new Ford crest emblem. In the case of the Tilt Cabs, this "Super-Duty" trim flanked the Ford crest that was centered between the headlights.

Ford also offered as options for this year heavier-duty axles that would allow a truck to carry a higher GVW or GCW rating. For ex-

Maeystown, Illinois, is where you can find this 1959 Ford F-750 fire truck with its 500-gpm Towers Body. Note the front mounted pump on this unit. *Dennis J. Maag Photo*

American LaFrance supplied the 1250-gpm pump body used on this 1960 Ford Super-Duty fire truck. This unit was based at the Amoco Refinery in Wood River, Illinois, before that facility closed. *Dennis J. Maag Photo*

ample, an F-750 model might use the same axles as say an F-800 or an F-850, which would allow it to carry a higher payload. The truck could do as much work as a heavier version but do it at a lower cost and maybe better fuel economy. Ford also offered higher-rated springs and shocks for buyers who just wanted a tougher truck. They also offered lots of other optional equipment so a buyer could "tailor make" a truck better suited to handle a certain job.

All Ford trucks in 1960 had their wiring improved and Super-Duty models came with thermostatically-controlled shutters mounted in front of their radiators to help their engines reach normal operating temperature sooner,

thus adding to their fuel economy numbers. These trucks also featured heavy-duty, double channel frames.

Ford didn't offer a tandem axle version of their "C" Tilt Cab models as a normal production model. However, if a buyer really needed a Tilt Cab Ford with a tandem axle setup, Ford would put one together under a special order basis.

When all was said and done, this era of Ford trucks had a tough road to follow after the popular 1953-1956 "Economy Trucks" that they replaced. However, Ford was up to the challenge and when this era was over Ford trucks were even more popular than they had been before.

A Custom Cab heavy-duty 1960 Ford dump truck sits abandoned in a construction yard in Arizona along with some other construction trucks.

One of the new features found on the 1960 Fords was a stylized rendition of a new Ford truck crest. This particular example was found in a dusty parts box found in a Midwest Ford dealership a couple of years ago.

Are you looking for a heavy-duty Ford wrecker for pulling big trucks? Then this Super-Duty Ford tow truck ought to fit the bill rather nicely.

1961-1964
Forging Ahead with some New Trucks

1961

Ford started out this new decade of the 1960s with a lineup of redesigned trucks and some new models that they hadn't offered before. These new models were found at the light-duty end as well as at the top end extra heavy-duty segment. The former was a new line of economy trucks called aptly, the "Econoline," while the latter was the "H" Series of semi tractors with the "H" standing for highway trucks. In between these two extremes was found a total redesign of Ford's bread-and-butter F Series line.

That redesign included a new cab that was a little wider and a little longer than the previous cab, and had a lot more glass area as well. It used a new styled hood that was a little wider, but at the same time flatter than the hood used on 1957-1960 models, and had more rounded sides as well. This cab also featured new doors, which were more rounded off than the old doors and used a deep character line that helped to integrate the front end of the truck to the back of the cab.

In addition, the front fenders were restyled on these trucks and the fenders used on the heavy-duty units were larger, more massive-looking bolt-on units. Once again the light-duty and medium-duty trucks had a different front-end design than the design used on the heavier-rated trucks. The bigger trucks used different front bumpers, and as a different styling approach, the new Ford F Series heavy-duty trucks were designed without grilles. These trucks featured a massive grille cavity, but instead of a grille they used large extruded metal panels that flanked the radiator. These large panels housed single headlamps that were trimmed with a beauty ring. Trucks equipped with Super-Duty engines had shutters installed in front of the radiator. When these shutters were closed, the shutters looked like they were part of the extruded grille panels.

Another difference noted on these new heavy-duty Ford trucks was the way their hoods fit on top of the fenders and the front grille panel. There was a noticeable gap that was probably put there to get more air flowing into the engine compartment to help in cooling. The heavy-duty front bumpers were slotted to help get air to flow past the front brakes.

As far as Tilt Cabs were concerned, the 1961-model year showed them going back to a single headlight system, which made the trucks look like the 1957 models again. A new option for these trucks was a fiberglass bolt-on sleeper compartment that was mounted to the back-side of the cab covering the rear window area. This sleeper compartment could be had with a 7-foot long foam pad mattress, or for a little more money a box spring type of mattress was available.

Moving up the ladder to the top of Ford's truck line for this year, a new series was founded. This new series was called the "H" Series and it comprised a grouping of high Tilt Cab models that were designed for over-the-

Judging by the trim on this heavy-duty dump truck, it is a 1961-1963 model. The owner thought the truck was a 1961 model and he still uses this truck in his landscaping business.

A new Ford H Series tractor with a diesel engine sits between a COE GMC and an old International conventional truck in this photo. *Bill Miller Collection*

road tractor/trailer work. The H Series, which consisted of 102 models, was basically a truck that used a Tilt Cab body that was shared with Ford's C Series. Where the two trucks differed was in truck height. The C Series were mounted low on the chassis while the H Series Tilt Cabs were mounted on top of a panel, which was mounted higher on its chassis. That separation panel was made up of a painted extruded metal that wrapped around the front of the truck and continued back along the sides of the cab to the backside.

The C Series Tilt Cabs also used large wheelwells cut into the side of the cab while the H Series trucks had the same area closed off, giving a smoother look to the sides of their cabs.

The H Series, as we stated at the start of this chapter, were made for highway tractor duty and this high-mounted cab allowed their drivers a better view of the road ahead. However, in order to get into this cab some help was needed. To alleviate this problem, Ford put a step in the separation panel and added a small ladder to both sides of the cab behind the doors. Like the C Series Tilt Cabs, a sleeper compartment option was available for the H Series trucks as well.

All of these Ford trucks were available as Standard or Custom Cab models. As before, the Custom Cab versions had a more upscale look to them.

Ford didn't stop with just the changes mentioned so far. They made quite a few more changes underneath these trucks as well. They featured new, stronger frames, a double channel type for straight trucks, and an extra high tensile strength steel single channel type for trucks used as tractor/trailer rigs. Heavier springs, larger brakes, and wider track front axles were also fitted to these new Fords. Also, higher-rated rear axles were available, allowing Ford to increase GVW ratings on some of these new trucks.

For the first time, Ford offered warranties on their new trucks in 1961. A 100,000-mile

This 1961-1963 Ford Tilt Cab C Series tractor was a pretty fancy truck back then. Its red and white combination made for a striking looking truck.

warranty was placed on Ford's heavy-duty super-duty engines for this year. This engine warranty covered parts that were worn out or defective through normal use in 100,000 miles. As an added bonus, a 12,000-mile warranty was offered on all Ford trucks built in 1961.

Another first for Ford truck buyers in 1961 was the option of choosing either a gasoline- or diesel-fueled powerplant for their trucks. The diesel engines were supplied to Ford by Cummins and were offered in the H Series of trucks. If one didn't want a diesel in this type of truck, Ford offered one of their Super-Duty V-8 gasoline engines. If an H Series truck was equipped with a diesel engine, it wore a "Diesel" crest emblem on the front of the cab.

When all was said and done Ford's 1961 truck lineup was the most changed and most extensive of any model lineup that had ever been offered by Ford prior to this time. The truck buying public showed how much they appreciated Ford's efforts by purchasing some 340,000 Ford trucks in 1961.

1962/1963

Ford made some minor changes to their trucks in 1962, but that certainly wasn't the case in 1963. Ford went all out to increase their share of the truck market segments they competed in that year. Chief among the changes noted in the Ford truck line in 1963 was the introduction of still another new series of Ford trucks. This new series was called the "N" Series and it consisted of a number of new medium and heavy-duty models. These trucks were basically short-nosed conventional trucks that fit between the F and C Series of trucks. The N Series of trucks featured an 89-inch BBC length, which was 7 inches longer than a comparable C model, but 13 inches shorter than an F Series truck. The N Series trucks used a high-mounted conventional F Series cab combined with a shorter hood, unique front fend-

This Ford Super-Duty F Series tandem axle tractor has a unique, weighted front bumper. Evidently, weights were added to the front bumper to keep the front end down when it pulled a heavy load.

Pueblo, Colorado, is the place where you'll find this restored Super-Duty F Series fire truck. It is painted white with gold lettering, red wheels, and red pin stripes.

Dennis Maag tells us this 1962 Ford F-800 fire truck is considered a tanker rather than a pumper. It once served in the Prairie Dupont Fire Protection District in Illinois. *Dennis J. Maag Collection*

ers, and a front end treatment that was similar to an F Series heavy-duty truck.

The new N Series Ford trucks weren't the only big news coming out of the Ford truck works for this year. Another big announcement by Ford concerned the expanded use of Cummins diesel powerplants in all models other than H Series trucks. Now, a Ford truck buyer could get a Cummins in an F, T, C, and N Series truck, both in six-cylinder or V-8 engine forms. Ford even expanded the diesel engine option down into their medium series rated trucks. Instead of that engine being a Cummins, the medium-duty "city diesels" used an engine built by Ford of Great Britain. When a diesel engine was specified for a truck, a "Diesel" crest was fitted to the front of the truck in everything but an F Series truck. In the case of an F Series truck that "Diesel" crest was placed on the side of the hood.

We found this 1962 Ford H Series tractor in a New Mexico junkyard back in the late 1980s. Note that this truck is powered by a diesel engine and has a sleeper unit.

This N Series Ford truck was found on the side of a mountain in Arizona. It is in pretty good shape considering that it has been sitting there for a while.

Ford made some wiring changes to their 1963 trucks and they came up with a new painting system that dipped their truck bodies in a special primer, which made them more rust resistant. Ford also improved their truck warranty coverage for 1963 by bumping up the coverage to 24,000 miles or 24 months, whichever came first.

1964

For 1964 Ford introduced a new series of FE "Big Block" gasoline truck engines. These engines were designed to be used for trucks right from the start rather than being modified car engines. These engines displaced 330, 361, and 391 cubic inches. All of these engines, except for the light-duty 330, were meant to replace the 302 and 332-cubic-inch engines used before. Speaking of engines, Ford made some changes in the line of diesel engines they offered for this year.

Other changes made by Ford included an alternator in place of a generator used in heavy-duty applications, and a center point steering front axle was made available on some heavy-duty models as well.

In 1963 Ford introduced their N Series of trucks. Here we see a heavy-duty tandem axle N Series wrecker parked beside a later model L Series unit.

Another N Series Ford truck sits outside a New Mexico truck terminal in the late 1980s.

This well worn 1961-1963 Ford Super-Duty F-850 dump truck looks like a retired highway department refugee. It now sits retired under a grove of trees on Myron Felix's place in Minnesota.

This F-750 fire truck has a lot of heavy-duty equipment associated with it. It is equipped with a Super-Duty engine, hood ventiports, and some heavy-duty wheels. *Bill Miller Collection*

These arrow-like hood trim pieces were used on 1961-1963 F Series Ford trucks. This piece is marked as a Super-Duty F-850.

For fighting fires in tall buildings you need a fire truck with an expandable platform for fire fighters to stand on like the unit shown here on a Ford Super-Duty truck. *Bill Miller Collection*

This Super-Duty Ford dump truck looks like a 1964 or 1965 model. It was found with a "For Sale" sign in its window in early 2000 in Colorado.

The Colorado Highway Department once owned and operated this heavy-duty N Series truck in southern Colorado along the I-25 corridor.

Look closely and you'll notice that this Ford Tilt Cab fire truck is not a Ford but a Canadian-built Mercury. It has been fitted out with a King Seagrave pump body. *Dennis J. Maag Photo*

Ford Experiments with Turbine

Ford made some big news literally when they debuted a super truck experimental model that hit the highways during a national road tour during the 1964 year. The truck was officially called "Ford's Gas Turbine" truck and it was basically a one-off exercise to show what Ford could offer the trucking industry in the future.

Nicknamed "Big Red" because it was big and painted red with gold accents, it had a 600 horsepower gasoline turbine engine that was hooked to a special modified 5-speed Allison automatic transmission.

It featured a futuristic-looking design, which was the brainchild of Ford's design, engineering, and scientific labs. It had a lightweight, fiberglass cab that stood 13 feet in height. It was made to be that tall so its top would be in line with the two 13-foot high trailers it pulled. By having tractor and trailers the same height, the airflow across them was much smoother, resulting in good fuel economy numbers.

This was a truck that was equipped with just about any equipment you could think of to make the driver and crew more comfortable. It had an oven, refrigerator, air conditioning, a sleeping compartment, and comfortable seating for its crew of three men. The drivers who had a chance to drive this vehicle were amazed how quiet and smooth it was compared to their regular trucks. It's a shame that this truck never made it into regular production because it probably would have revolutionized the industry. This special truck was retired after its national tour and in the late-1970s it appeared in a "garage sale" catalog for the Holman and Moody racing shops. As far as anybody knows it hasn't been seen since.

When we found this fire engine in Marysville, Kansas, it had just come out of the body shop where it had been repainted.

This photo shows a new W Series Ford tractor pulling a couple of trailers. This photo was taken soon after these trucks were introduced. *Ford Motor Company Photo*

1965-1969
Increasing Market Share by Offering More Trucks

1965

The mid- to late-1960s was an exciting time to be in the trucking business for the Ford Motor Company. They were coming out with more new models to fit a wider variety of trucking jobs and they were constantly improving their bread-and-butter models to make them even more appealing. The trucking market was getting more competitive with each passing year and products had to be better than the next guy's or you were quickly left behind.

For 1965, Ford made quite a few improvements to their cabs to make them more comfortable to the driver and his passengers. In the early part of the model year they added some extra insulation in the cabs to make them quieter and at the same time they added some reinforcements to the cabs to make them stronger and more resistant to flexing. Ford also used some zinc-based primers on the underbody areas to make them more resistant to rusting out.

Other changes seen on these early model 1965 Ford trucks were heavier-duty axles, transmissions, rear ends, and reinforced frames to make the trucks tougher. Transistorized ignition systems were offered as optional equipment for this year on 330, 361, 391, 401, 477, and 534-cubic-inch engines. These ignitions helped to provide hotter spark at high rpm levels, which kept the power up when it was needed the most.

Ford came out with a new model for this year as well and it was called a T-8000. It was basically a tandem axle truck with a diesel powerplant. Also, a new Caterpillar diesel engine was now available for Ford's H Series trucks on a special order basis. This engine displaced some 525 cubic inches and put out 220 horsepower at 2200 rpm. The torque rating was a powerful 587 lbs/ft at a low 1700 rpm. It had lots of pulling power for sure.

Towards the end of the 1965 model year, on or about July 12, 1965, Ford made some major cab revisions to their conventional F, T, and N

Series trucks—revisions that made these cabs look different from Ford's earlier cabs. The major change noted on these trucks was their raised roof panels. The new roof panels stood 3 1/2 inches higher than similar cabs used before, and added some much-needed extra headroom inside these cabs.

Ford didn't just change the roof panels in these trucks. They also raised the seat track height by 2 1/2 inches, which gave some extra legroom and a more comfortable seating position. Above the driver, Ford added a molded fiberglass headliner that gave the roof area a more finished appearance.

Besides raising the roof and changing the seat mounts, Ford also repositioned the steering column, which gave the steering wheel a flatter position. A bigger steering wheel was also featured in these trucks and made them easier to steer and maneuver in tight situations.

Original 1965 Suggested Retail Truck Prices

Series	Wheelbase	Model	Price
C-800	135 inches	Chassis/Cab	$6,939.12
T-750	176 inches	Chassis/Cab	$8,158.24
T-800	176 inches	Chassis/Cab	$9,152.01
CT-800	153 inches	Chassis/Cab	$10,887.65
B-750	260.5 inches	Chassis/Cowl	$4,228.87
F-850	158 inches	Chassis/Cab	$7,078.39
F-950	176 inches	Chassis/Cab	$7,581.85
F-1000	176 inches	Chassis/Cab	$9,077.30
F-1100	176 inches	Chassis/Cab	$9,970.53
N-950	158 inches	Chassis/Cab	$7,812.19
N-1000	134 inches	Chassis/Cab	$8,958.58
N-1100	158 inches	Chassis/Cab	$9,909.55
F-950-D	158 inches	Chassis/Cab	$12,482.10
F-1000-D	176 inches	Chassis/Cab	$12,861.53
F-1100-D	176 inches	Chassis/Cab	$13,754.45
N-950-D	158 inches	Chassis/Cab	$13,638.90
N-1000-D	158 inches	Chassis/Cab	$14,048.33
N-1100-D	158 inches	Chassis/Cab	$14,941.55
C-950	99 inches	Chassis/Cab	$8,837.48
C-1000	135 inches	Chassis/Cab	$10,010.93
C-1100	135 inches	Chassis/Cab	$10,093.85
T-850	158 inches	Chassis/Cab	$9,746.21
T-950	158 inches	Chassis/Cab	$12,481.83
NT-850	158 inches	Chassis/Cab	$9,961.12
NT-950	158 inches	Chassis/Cab	$12,525.23
T-850-D	176 inches	Chassis/Cab	$16,2555.48
NT-850-D	158 inches	Chassis/Cab	$16,249.48
NT-950-D	176 inches	Chassis/Cab	$17,421.86
H-1000	158 inches	Chassis/Cab	$10,142.13
H-1000-D	158 inches	Chassis/Cab	$15,241.04

Ford used these "ventiports" in some hoods to help vent warm air out from under the hood.

1965 Prices (Popular Options)

Options	Prices
Custom Cab	$80.30
477 Super-duty V-8	$220.70 (850-950 trucks)
534 Super-duty V-8	$243.60 (1000-1100 trucks)
Tinted Windshield	$14.30
Brush Type Grille Guard	$28.00
Deluxe Fresh Air Heater	$86.50
Transistorized Ignition	$67.70
Warning Lamps	$33.10 (heat, oil, water)
Aluminum Wheels	$104.20 (10 studs)
Power Steering	$255.80 (7000-9000 lb front axle)
22 inch Steering Wheel	$5.70
Tractor Frame	$13.50 (80,000 PSI)
Reinforced Frame	$28.50 (50,000 PSI)
Saddle Tanks	$227.40 (125 gallons)
Dual Electric Horn	$9.40
Western Type Mirrors	$39.30
Two-tone Paint	$17.00
Power Take Off	$103.00 (crankshaft mounted)
Manual Radio	$62.30
Bostrom Driver's Seat	$104.00 (Standard Cab)
Bostrom Driver's Seat	$72.10 (Custom Cab)
Safety Package	$20.60 (padded dash, padded visors)
Tractor Package	$249.10 (air brakes required)
Fuller 10-speed R-96 Transmission	$1,004.50
Transmatic Auto Trans	$1,131.60
Air/Hydraulic Combination Brakes	$315.4

Larry Jones owns this great looking 1966 F-850 Super-Duty fire engine. This fire engine was fitted with a NAPCO four-wheel drive conversion so that it could be taken off road to fight fires in a rural area. *Judy Jones Photo*

Want to see what a Standard Cab H Series interior looks like. Check out Bill Wasner's 1965 H-950 truck.

The H Series Ford is a tall truck as you can plainly see. Getting into the cab presents a unique set of problems, so Ford wisely added a ladder and grab handles to make it easier to climb up into these cabs.

This is the Super-Duty emblem that Ford used on their H Series trucks in the mid-1960s.

Another look at an H Series Ford truck interior showing the dashboard, instrument cluster, steering wheel, and column.

Bill Wasner, of Saint Joseph, Minnesota, owns and restored this 1965 H-950 tractor that he originally bought for $65.00. It was in a lot worse shape when he picked it up and brought it home.

Below. Ford's H Series tractors were some of the best looking trucks on the road back in the 1960s. It's too bad that we don't see more of them on the road today, like this auto parts tractor/ trailer combination. *Dick Copello Collection*

1966

As was mentioned in the beginning of this chapter, Ford was always trying to improve these trucks and that claim was true for the 1966 model year. Take the C Series for instance. Ford updated these trucks with a new steering gear that reduced steering effort. The C Series Tilt Cabs also were fitted with a new, 4-inch wider front axle, which moved the tires and wheels closer to the outside of the wheelwells and resulted in a more stable handling system.

For buyers who wanted diesel engines Ford offered three new Cummins engines. These engines were called the NHC 250 Cummins and they all differed in horsepower ratings. The lowest engine was rated at 225 horsepower at 1950 rpm, the next at 225 horsepower at 2100 rpm, and the highest one rated at 250 horsepower

The Warrenville, Illinois, Fire Protection District owns this neat 1966 Ford Super-Duty F-850 with an Alexis 750-gpm pump body. *Dennis J. Maag Photo*

You will find this 1967 C-1000 Ford fire truck at the Missouri Eastern Correctional Center in Pacific, Missouri. This unit features a Young-built body that can pump about 750 gallons of water per minute. *Dennis J. Maag Photo*

The Red, White, and Blue Fire Department of Breckenridge, Colorado, keeps this 1969 Ford F Series Super-Duty in reserve status. The unit is fitted with a NAPCO 4-wheel drive conversion so that it can climb mountain roads in any type of weather situation. *Dennis J. Maag Photo*

at 2100 rpm. If you didn't want to run a diesel but wanted to run a cleaner fuel than gasoline, Ford offered an option on some of their truck engines that would allow them to run on liquefied petroleum gas.

Other new features found on 1966 Fords included new tandem rear suspension systems, larger air brakes on some models, higher capacity tires, a "Million Mile" odometer on F-800 and higher trucks, 16-gauge electrical wiring, and higher-rated front axles.

In May of 1966 Ford's H Series trucks came to the end of their road. Ford still wanted to have a truck in this end of the market so they came out with a new model to replace the H Series trucks. This new model was called the "W" Series, and like the H Series trucks it replaced, this was a high-mounted Tilt Cab-type truck.

This tall cab truck featured a wide, square-looking design that was a bit plainer looking than the H Series trucks they replaced. It was a unique cab that wasn't shared with any other Ford truck. It had a large, two-piece windshield and, like the C Series Tilt Cabs, it had a short BBC (Bumper to Back of Cab) length of 52 inches which made it perfect for tractor/trailer duties. The cab featured a high-strength, all-steel welded construction that was mounted atop a fiberglass separation lower panel. The cab could be tilted some 55 degrees for regular repair work or it could be tilted a full 80 degrees for major repairs and the like.

Unlike the H Series models the W Series trucks were only available with diesel engines. However, there were quite a few diesel engines available from which to choose, including Cummins, Caterpillar, and Detroit Diesel engines.

These trucks came equipped with lots of standard equipment that was optional on similar trucks from other manufacturers. It had equipment like a full complement of illuminated Stewart Warner gauges, separate heater and air conditioning ducting, insulated color-coded wiring, zinc-based paint primers, tinted glass throughout the cab, and an isolated vertical snorkel air intake and separate exhaust system to reduce noise and vibrations from coming into the cab.

Ford Experiments with Turbine Again

In late 1966 Ford decided to once again test the Turbine Waters, but instead of producing a "one-off" special show truck like "Big Red," this time around Ford decided to just drop a turbine engine into their new W Series trucks.

The turbine engine chosen for this test was another Ford engineering prototype called the "707." This engine was dropped into about a dozen W Series "mules," tractors that pulled trailers that hauled parts between Ford plants in the Midwest. By being in the Ford Factory Fleet, these trucks could be put through the normal day-to-day routine that is the trucking business.

Period reports of these trucks showed them to be a lot quieter than regular diesel engine trucks, a lot lighter to handle, and smoother to run in all aspects associated with moving cargo loads. These engines were a lot smaller and lighter than regular diesel engines but they put out more power and had fuel economy numbers that compared quite favorably with diesels.

Ford's test results showed that their Turbine Engine Program was successful and this being the case, one would wonder why we don't see turbines in general use today. That probably has something to do with costs and the industry's preference for diesel power. However, if the federal government persists in their goal to clean up diesel emissions, the turbine engine may make a comeback.

Looking for a different Ford to restore? How about picking up this N Series Ford tractor that has been sitting in northern New Mexico with a For Sale sign on it for a number of years?

1967

For the year of 1967 there was really no big news that involved heavy-duty trucks at Ford. Most of the news revolved around a new styling job that was done on light and medium-duty F Series trucks. These trucks featured a new slab-sided look that looked neat especially when done on the medium-duty heavy trucks that Ford was pushing for this year to get a bigger share of this market segment. Basically, a medium-duty heavy Ford truck was a medium-duty truck that was fitted with heavy-duty parts to boost its ratings. The beauty of this arrangement was the truck buyer got a heavy-duty truck for the price of a medium-duty one.

A New Mexico tractor dealer used this Super-Duty Ford F Series truck to haul his tractors around the state. Note "Super-Duty" hood scoop, air horns, and air conditioning box mounted on the roof.

Old Ford trucks don't die, they just keep going from job to job. This unit we found sitting outside a garage in Wisconsin last summer.

Let us not forget some of the great looking school buses that Ford built during the late 1960s and early 1970s. This unit, wearing a chrome-plated grille, looks to be a 1967 heavy-duty model.

1968

As far as heavy-duty and higher-rated trucks, 1968 saw mostly minor changes to Ford's lineup of trucks.

These changes included new federally mandated side marker lights, interior trim changes, and changes in exterior trim pieces. Ford did expand their diesel engine offerings this year and also made some changes to their truck frames to give them higher ratings. They also made changes in their braking systems. Also, as an extra cost option, a W Series truck buyer could order an aluminum cab version to give them a lighter truck.

1969

Changes again were minimal in 1969 on Ford heavy-duty and extra heavy-duty trucks and the reason for this might have had something to do with the fact that Ford was planning on making some really major changes in their 1970 model lineup. With the introduction of these new trucks some of Ford's heavy-duty models would cease to exist, some of them dating back to the late 1950s.

Though they aren't seen anymore, in some parts of the country there are still a lot of N Series Ford trucks waiting to be found out there.

Myron Felix thinks that this N Series truck of his might be one of the last trucks of its kind to come down the assembly line. He bought this 1969 model in early 1970.

Below. Looking for a very rare Ford truck? You might want to check out this Ford truck we spotted in Bill Wasner's Ford truck parts yard. It is, according to what Bill tells us, a one-off Ford F Series truck with a removable backhoe mounted on its chassis. This was an experimental truck built by the combined efforts of Ford's Truck and Tractor Divisions.

Ford added a little extra brightness to the look of their
L Series trucks in 1971 when a brushed aluminum
grille and grille surround were offered.

1970-1975
Louisville Line Leads the Way

1970

If you remember the late 1960s you'll probably recall Ford's light bulb "Better Idea" promotional campaigns. Well, in the trucking world, Ford's best idea of that period was the release of a new line of trucks that came from a new truck assembly plant located just outside Louisville, Kentucky. The truck was called the "Louisville Line" and the rest, as they say, is Ford truck history. For 29 years the Louisville Line made up a great deal of Ford truck history. It was one of the most popular and most famous Ford trucks of all time.

Getting back to the beginning the Louisville Line, or L Series for short, was the first truck off the line at Ford's then new Kentucky Truck Plant. The time was late-1969 and the truck was a brand new 1970 model.

The Louisville Line was a new series of trucks for Ford that consisted of medium, heavy-duty, and extra heavy-duty trucks. With the release of this new series of trucks Ford was able to do away with their N Series, T Series, and heavy-duty F Series trucks. These trucks filled a wide variety of jobs from city deliveries to over-the-road line haul duties.

These were great-looking trucks that didn't look like anything else on the road at that time. They featured wide, roomy steel cabs with steel reinforced fiberglass tilting front ends. Or, if you wanted, an optional butterfly style opening hood was available. Getting into the cab itself, they were roomy with lots of headroom, good legroom, and comfortable chair high seating. That chair high seating faced an instrument panel that curved around a bit so that all its easy-to-read gauges could be scanned by the driver in short spans of time so that he could keep his eyes on the road ahead. Also, there was an adjustable steering column that was available to make the steering wheel position more comfortable for the driver.

Another feature found in these cabs were the air controls that were shaped in such a fashion that allowed a driver to set them by feel without having to look at them before making a move. These controls were connected to color-coded nylon lines. This color-coding allowed for easier tracing in case a problem developed. Green-colored lines were for the primary system, red-colored for the secondary system, orange for the parking system, and yellow for accessories.

Ford's big news in the 1970 model year was their new L Series, or Louisville Line, of trucks. This early model tandem axle dump truck has been in Myron Felix's fleet since it was new.

This 1970s-era Ford C model Tilt Cab tractor is a tow vehicle for the Albuquerque Fire Department. They use it to tow a trailer that hauls their antique fire engine.

Some F Series Ford trucks, like this tractor trailer rig, were equipped with heavy-duty parts in the 1970s. This Custom Cab model has a lot of brightwork adorning it.

Another item of note found on these trucks (made to cut down on electrical problems) was the placement of four easy-to-reach junction blocks with easy-to-plug and unplug connectors. These cabs were also placed on premium steel frames with a high tensile rating, in single or double channel styles.

The L Series trucks were available as short or long conventional models with the short ones featuring a BBC (bumper to back of cab) dimension of 93.3 inches, while the BBC for the long models was 105.3 inches. They were also available with a wide selection of gasoline or diesel engine choices and the same can be said for transmissions and rear ends as well. There were lots of other options to "tailor make" these trucks to handle just about any job that one could imagine.

This early model Ford L Series truck is one of the few that came with a non-tilting front end. Probably because it had a power take off (pto) unit working through a hole under the grille.

This Ford L Series truck was found outside Center Ford in Center, Colorado. It is equipped with some sort of agricultural body.

1971

The only real news that concerned the 1971 Ford heavy-duty truck line was the availability of a set back front axle. The models equipped with these axles carried an "S" in their model designation like "LTS-9000" with the "S" meaning setback axle. The beauty of such an arrangement was that these trucks could carry a higher payload because the relocated axle could support more of the extra weight. A lot of these trucks were used in the construction industry. Other changes made on these 1971 trucks were mostly minor in nature.

1972

Ford followed the 1971 model year with a number of changes to their 1972 trucks. Starting off the list of changes was an RPO (Regular Production Option) double channel frame that featured all bolted construction. A full depth channel reinforcement ran the entire length of the frame on both sides. This frame had a high yield strength of 100,000 pounds per square inch rating. This frame was available for LT, LTS-8000, and LTS-9000 models. By having an all-bolted frame, new equipment could be added to the truck by just bolting it on.

Opposite page top. This US Air Force fire truck is a 1971 Ford 4x4 unit that once had a Ward LaFrance body on its chassis, but it now carries a later model Quality body. *Dennis J. Maag Photo*

Opposite page bottom. The Lake St. Louis Fire Protection District of Lake St. Louis, Missouri, owned this 1972 Ford L-900 fire truck until they sold it in 1998. It is equipped with a Firemaster Body and a cab enclosure. *Dennis J. Maag Photo*

This page top. A Ford W Series tractor sits in a field in New Mexico awaiting a new owner. Judging by the adjustable mirrors on this truck it was probably used as a mobile home mover.

Quite a few early model L Series trucks ended up as car hauler tractors like this truck with its load of used cars.

Hadley Auto Transport has had a contract to haul new Ford cars and trucks throughout the Western USA. Their blue and white trucks are a familiar sight on the highways and byways of this area.

Ford offered up a new cab in their Louisville Line this year. It was a cab with a concave rear cab panel, a panel that curved inward to provide extra clearance for a front mounted refrigeration unit on the front of a trailer or body. This cab had a BBC length of 90 inches and was referred to as the "Reefer" cab in Ford truck literature of the time.

For their W Series trucks in 1972 Ford wanted to boost their appeal to potential buyers and they did that by releasing three new W Series deluxe Owner/Operator Packages, which really added to their curb appeal. These packages offered the customer the chance to really personalize his or her truck. The first package came with a thick pile nylon carpet that was placed over a top-quality foam pad and a padded retaining rail if the truck had a sleeper compartment. These trucks also came with a chassis painted in body color, a bright finished front bumper, a body colored air intake tube, dual air horns mounted on the roof, and roof-mounted clearance lights. Other items included in this package were bright-plated vent window trim, and a bright finish on its West Coast Mirrors.

The second package was the Owner/Operator Exterior Paint Option, which included the choice of exterior color combinations and a graphics package. The last package was an exhaust system upgrade that consisted of a chrome-plated exhaust stack covered by a fiberglass padded stainless steel muffler. Some W and WT Series trucks this year were equipped with all three Owner/Operator Packages, which really made them stand out as eye catching, head turning trucks.

Another change to mention is in reference to exhaust systems. On the W and WT Series of trucks in this year Ford added rain caps to the top of all vertical exhaust stacks to keep rain from getting down into the intake passages of their diesel engines.

1973

A new Owner/Operator Package for the Louisville Line heralded the changes seen on the new-for-1973 Ford trucks. Items included in this new option were stainless steel West Coast mirrors, roof-mounted cab and clearance lights, dual 25-inch long air horns, padded door panels, wood-tone trim around gauges, special nylon carpet, a special plaque with the owner's name etched on it, chassis painted in body color, and special exterior color and graphic combinations to really make these trucks stand out from regular versions.

Midway through the 1973 model year Ford released a redesigned W Series line of trucks. These new trucks featured cabs with more rounded lines, which really made them look different than the trucks they replaced. Ford

Tilt Cab Fords were still pretty popular when this model was built. Though this truck is semi-retired now it can still do a full day's work.

Myron Felix bought one of Ford's W Series tractors for his fleet back in 1973. And that truck, shown here, is still being used in his fleet of trucks today.

redesigned these W Series trucks to be more aerodynamic so that they could move through the air with less resistance, which was of prime importance back in the fuel shortage days of 1973 (when fuel economy numbers were the number one concern of car and truck buyers).

These trucks also featured a new grille treatment that they shared with the Louisville Line trucks. The new "W" had a grille that featured an aluminum finish on the panel that surrounded it. Like the L Series trucks, this grille surround used a set of F O R D letters painted in black for identification purposes. A restyled front bumper also changed the looks of these trucks.

As a bonus to W Series truck buyers who were concerned about weight, Ford offered a lightweight version of this truck as an option for this year. This lightweight option consisted of the following lighter components: an all-aluminum cab, aluminum hubs and disc wheels, aluminum 60-gallon fuel tank, aluminum front bumper, horizontal exhaust system, front-wheel brake delete, centrifuge rear brake drums, Reyco 101 torque leaf rear springs, Page & Page

rear suspension system, Detroit Diesel engine, and a tandem rear axle setup (on tandem axle trucks) with aluminum carriers.

Like the W Series trucks they replaced, these redesigned W trucks were available in regular or sleeper cab versions, with single or tandem rear axles, and as a Standard Cab or as a deluxe Owner/Operator truck.

1974/1975

After making all these changes to their trucks in 1972 and 1973, Ford made only minor changes to their 1974 and 1975 models. For the former, changes were made in diesel engine choices offered by Ford. They also offered some new Louisville tandem axle models to their lineup and radial tires were offered as an option on some truck models for these years. For the C Series Tilt Cabs Ford added some wider wheel well lips, which made the trucks look a little different for these years. For the latter, 1975, urethane foam insulation replaced the fiberglass padding used previously. Due to a new federal mandate, all trucks with air brake systems for 1975 were required to be fitted with anti-skid mechanisms.

Castle Wood Fire Department of Castle Wood, Colorado, runs this 1974 Ford Series fire truck that is equipped with a locally built body. *Dennis J. Maag Photo*

A W Series Ford tractor with a car hauler trailer sits outside an auto auction facility waiting for its next load.

1976-1979
Closing out the 1970s

1976

Back in 1976 truck owners and operators were still concerned with fuel economy. The price of gasoline was high and more truck buyers were opting for diesel engines. The cost of diesel fuel was lower and since diesel engines offered as much power, if not more than gasoline engines, it was the only way to go for a number of truck buyers. Ford offered them a number of diesel engines from which to choose. As a matter of fact, the increased popularity of diesel engines caused Ford to drop their once popular 401-cubic-inch Super-duty gasoline engine during this year.

Ford offered three economy engines in their 9000 Series, which offered better fuel economy figures for this year. These engines were the Cummins Formula 290, the Caterpillar Economy 3406, and the Detroit Diesel 8V-71TT.

For those truck owners who were looking for a sleeker, longer conventional truck for line hauling work, Ford released a new model for the 1976 model year. This new model debuted in October 1975 and Ford called it their "LTL-9000 Series." The "LTL's" main claim to fame was that it was the longest Louisville truck that Ford ever produced. Its major feature was its nose, which measured a 13-inch increase in length over a standard Louisville. It also used a special squared-off grille shell, which was its most prominent feature. Its fiberglass tilting front end featured hood vents in the sides of its hood to help extricate hot air from the engine compartment.

This was Ford's "Big Daddy" model and it came with lots of standard equipment, which was optional on other trucks. It had equipment like dual 100-gallon fuel tanks, Unison Air-Ride driver's seat, an adjustable steering column, maintenance-free 80-amp-hour batteries, dual air cam brakes, Kelsey-Hayes Anti Skid braking system, tinted glass, Unison passenger seat, wood-tone instrument panel cover, nylon carpeted interior, bright-plated exhaust stack, buffed aluminum grille and surround, dual chrome-plated air horns, stainless steel West Coast mirrors, torpedo-shaped clearance lights, body color painted frame, aluminum front bumper, Owner/Operator door-mounted trim plaque, bright-plated hood latches, assist handles, windshield trim band, and the choice of a dozen tri-color exterior paint combinations. With all this equipment is it any wonder why this truck became Ford's standard bearer?

The LTL cab was available in two BBC configurations, a 118.3-inch standard cab and a 154.3-inch sleeper cab version. Wheelbases on these trucks ranged from 174 inches to 246, making this, as was previously mentioned, the longest Ford truck offered at that time.

The LTL-9000 was powered by a diesel engine, usually a Cummins NTC-350 that was backed up by a Fuller RT 10-speed Roadranger transmission. It was also equipped with all three of Ford's Owner/Operator Packages. As such it was, in a few words, Ford's biggest, baddest, and best-equipped truck that ever came out of Louisville.

1977

For 1977 Ford made a few improvements across the board to make their trucks even more appealing to truck buyers. One thing that was new with the Louisville Line, or L Series, was that Ford now offered a set back front axle on L-800, L-8000, L-900, and L-9000 models. Previously, a set back front axle was only offered on tandem rear axle models. This new series of Louisville trucks was called Ford's "LS" Series, with the "S" standing for set back front axle model.

With the addition of these "LS" trucks, Ford was expanding their L Series trucks at the same time they were consolidating some models in their "C," "F," and even in the lower ranks of their Louisville Line. So, the total number of Ford trucks stayed about the same.

Once again the "LTL-9000" was Ford's "Big Daddy" conventional truck with the "W" and "C" Series trucks still being the biggest Tilt Cab versions. On the "W" Series truck Ford offered an air ride cab suspension that helped to cushion the ride by cutting down vibrations coming

This beautiful 1976 Ford F-750 fire truck with a Firemaster body belongs to the DeSoto Rural Fire Protection District of DeSoto, Missouri. *Dennis J. Maag Photo*

inside. The system consisted of self-leveling air springs, shock absorbers, and control arms, which allowed the cab to move about independently in relationship to the movements of the chassis.

Ford offered more maintenance-free batteries this year and more modular electrical and air brake system components for easier servicing or replacement. They also offered a new optional speed control system that allowed for better fuel economy numbers in some trucks.

At the end of this model year Ford's "W" Series trucks came to the end of its line if you'll excuse the pun ("W" Series of Linehaulers). The "W" Series had served Ford well for eleven years but this area of the market was calling for more stylish trucks. Ford had one waiting in the wings, ready, willing, and able to pick up where the "W" Fords left off.

Judging by their orange color these L Series Ford dump trucks are ex highway department trucks. We found these two sitting in an International used truck lot in Minneapolis, Minnesota.

Below. This Elwood Fire Protection District 1976 Ford C Series truck has been equipped with a 1977 Alexis body. Note how the cab on this fire truck has been modified to add more seating capacity. *Dennis J. Maag Photo*

Not all Ford fire trucks look like Fords. Case in point
is this 1977 Gerstenlager fire rescue body on a 1977
Ford truck chassis. *Dennis J. Maag Photo*

This 1977 Ford C Cab fire truck features a 1978
Towers body. Dennis Maag tells us that in 1990 or so
this truck was retrofitted to accept the cab enclosure
seen behind the cab. *Dennis J. Maag Photo*

1978

The biggest news at Ford for the 1978 model year concerned the "W" Series replacement that Ford called the CL-9000. Before we get to detailing this new Ford, let us digress a moment and discuss a milestone event that happened at the Ford Motor Company in 1978. This year was the year that Ford celebrated their 75th Anniversary. This celebration was a lot more involved than the 50th Anniversary, which Ford celebrated in 1953, but it will probably pale in comparison to Ford's 100th, which will be held in 2003.

Getting back to the new CL-9000, as we said, was Ford's biggest news of the 1978 model year. This truck was Ford's standard bearer into the top end of the linehauler end of the business. It was designed to go toe-to-toe with Freightliner's and Kenworth's best premium units. It was a quality product that looked every bit the part from the smallest part found on the frame to the deluxe air horns mounted on its tall cab.

This truck was full of neat features that weren't found on any other Ford truck or on other maker's trucks for that matter. Features like a welded aluminum cab and a climate control system with individual controls for the driver, passenger, and sleeper unit, if so equipped. That sleeper compartment also featured a circulating air system under the sleeper platform, which helped to keep the sleeper bed warm. Other features included a molded structural foam instrument panel with heavy-duty instrument circuitry with plug in units that got their power from a buss bar. There was also a

Rear three quarter view of a 1970s L Series short wheelbase tractor. This truck looks like it just came out of the paint shop.

Trinidad, Colorado, is where you'll find this sharp looking 1978 Ford F Series white over red fire truck.

It still looks good today, 22 years after it joined the fire department.

nifty serviceable air manifold system that could be easily removed and repaired or replaced to help reduce downtime. This system also had quick connect fittings on the air lines, making it faster to replace and reducing downtime. Reducing downtime keeps the truck on the road longer, helping to increase its potential for making profits, and making profits is what the trucking business is all about.

Up front these trucks used forged aluminum axles that were rated at 12,000 pounds per square inch and on their backends they used lightweight Reyco tandem axle setups on CLT-9000 trucks. Frames were made of high strength steel or aluminum and their frame rails featured all bolted construction. Their fuel tanks were also made of aluminum and their springs featured "lubed-for-life" pins holding them in their hangers.

These trucks were designed from the ground up with three types of cabs. A non-sleeper straight cab, a sleeper cab with a narrow sleeper unit, and a deep sleeper unit. The CL-9000 cab came in five lengths. There was a 54-inch BBC cab, a 64-inch BBC cab in the non-sleeper variety, a 76-inch BBC sleeper cab (with 24-inch wide bed), an 88-inch BBC sleeper cab (with a 32-inch wide bed), and a 110-inch BBC sleeper (with a 54-inch wide bed). These cabs came in a choice of 20 solid exterior colors, 12 glamour colors, and 36 combination colors.

These cabs also featured large, two-piece wraparound windshields that covered more than 2,592 square inches of area. It was more than enough room to give an ample view of the road ahead, and because these cabs were so tall, the driver of one of these trucks could get an unobstructed view of the road ahead with enough time to keep the driver out of trouble.

Inside these cabs Ford didn't scrimp on the comfort and convenience equipment and they didn't cut corners by using cheap materials. Ford used high-quality materials throughout these trucks. The interiors of the trucks were set up to be an efficient work environment for driver and passenger alike. A full complement of gauges were placed in front of the driver with switches and controls placed in a panel to the

Here we see a two-tone painted W Series Ford tractor with a cut down front bumper. This truck looks like it's been working for a very long time.

Opposite page bottom.
Check out that "v" plow sitting on the front end of this Louisville tandem axle dump truck. It is waiting for the first winter snow to get back to work.

right of the driver. Two seats were placed in the cab separated by a low engine doghouse cover. In standard cab form a rubber mat was placed over a 7/8-inch layer of sound proofing material. Base level interiors also came with perforated vinyl trim panels on the cab's backside, on the side panels, as well as the headliner. There was also lots of legroom and headroom in these cabs, adding to their comfort. If a deluxe cab was more to your liking, Ford offered the Hi-Level Owner/Operator Package A. This package included some unique trim panels that were done in a red, blue, or chamois color. There was also a brushed aluminum finish on the instrument cluster face and a 36-ounce premium color coordinated carpet was laid on the floor and on the doghouse cover. Seat trim was also color-coordinated, keeping with the luxurious theme.

In order for the driver to see out of the right hand side of the cab, an observation window was placed in the lower front door panel. There was another observation window placed in the lower rear part of the back panel on the right side of some cabs.

Base CL-9000 units featured large single headlights and mirrors, bumper, grille, and wheel splash moldings painted in a silver argent color. Also, F O R D letters were mounted between the two separate grille panels. If a truck buyer ordered the Exterior Package C, this grouping of equipment included a bright finish grille surround, West Coast mirrors in a bright-plated finish, chrome-plated, torpedo-shaped, roof-mounted clearance lights, aluminum front bumper, aluminum finish on the muffler stack and elbow, dual chrome-plated Grover air horns

mounted on the roof, bright-plated fuel tank caps, and stacked dual rectangular headlamps per side.

Ford's Owner/Operator trim packages were very popular at this time and the three packages offered for the CL-9000 and CLT-9000 were no exception. Package "A" included the following standard equipment: deluxe door trim panels, plush carpeting on the floor and doghouse cover, Bostrom Companion II seat, leather wrapped sport steering wheel, left hand reading lamp, right hand vanity mirror/lamp combination in sleeper compartment, and other goodies. Package "B" offered three different two-tone and tape striping exterior paint combinations. Package "C" included a Ford cloisonné emblem mounted between the two wiper panels, a bright finish on an aluminum front bumper, a bright finish on the muffler and exhaust system stack, dual rectangular stacked headlights per side, stainless steel West Coast mirrors, chrome-plated Grover deluxe air horns, chrome-plated torpedo shaped clearance lights, and a chrome-plated fuel tank cap.

These trucks were powered by high output Cummins KT and KTA engines with horsepower ratings of up to 600. Manual transmissions of 9-, 10-, and 13-speed helped to move all that power to a single, or tandem rear axle setup.

As mentioned before, these cabs were also available with an air suspension system as an option. This system, through the use of air bags, shock absorbers, and control arms, allowed the cab to move a bit, thus cutting down on noise and vibrations intruding into the cab environment.

Twenty color choices were available in single-tone exterior paint jobs. These trucks featured two coats of paint over two coats of primer. Optional at extra cost were Ford's "Glamour" paint finishes in a choice of twelve colors. Trucks with this paint option used a bonding coat of paint, two coats of primer, two coats of "glamour" paint, covered by two coats of clear acrylic enamel, for a total of seven different coats of paint to give them a glamourous, rich, high quality, exterior finish to make any driver proud. Frames on trucks with regular paint jobs were cleaned with a solvent and then painted in a primer coat. This was followed by two coats of baked black chassis enamel. Trucks with "Glamour" paint jobs had their frames painted the same, while trucks with the Owner/Operator "B" Package were painted in a color to compliment the cab's exterior color combinations.

If weight was a concern, Ford offered an extra cost, optional, Lightweight Package for these trucks. This package included an aluminum frame, aluminum fuel tanks, aluminum wheels, aluminum hubs, aluminum rear axle carriers, and aluminum suspension brackets.

1979

There wasn't much news to speak about as far as Ford trucks were concerned in the 1979 model year.

Things around the truck works were tame compared to all that was going on in the previous years. However, we did see some new Ford gasoline engines introduced in this year. These new engines were built at Ford's Lima, Ohio, engine plant. The engines, three of them, were a 370-cubic-inch V-8 with a 2V carburetor, a 370-cubic-inch V-8 with a 4V carburetor, and a 429-cubic-inch V-8 with a 4V carburetor. This was also the first year that Ford used a new marketing campaign that would stay with them for years. Ford called this new campaign their "Built Ford Tough" campaign. This year also brought to a close an era that saw Ford return to a leadership position in the trucking world, a role that they wouldn't relinquish for many years to come.

Opposite page. Another L Series tractor pulling a car trailer sits outside a truck terminal waiting to receive another load.

Air intake for diesel engines on the Ford L Series
trucks is provided by this circular plenum mounted
on the right side of the hood.

1980-1986
Staying the Course

1980

The big news at Ford's Truck Division starting out the 1980s decade involved new designs for Ford's light and medium-duty trucks. Changes on Ford's heavy-duty trucks were mostly minor in nature.

1981

There were a few changes made for 1981 meant to improve the performance of Ford's big trucks. In order to make their truck cabs more comfortable for the driver and passenger, Ford expanded the number of seat options offered. To get the trucks to stop better, Ford improved the braking systems of their heavy-duty trucks. To make the trucks look prettier, Ford added more colors and color combinations to their exterior paint palette. Self-adjustable and self-dampening clutches made maintenance easier and driving these trucks a little easier as well. Ford also expanded the number of transmissions and rear end choices for their heavy-duty trucks to make them perform better over a wider range of trucking jobs.

1982

Once again Ford made some minor changes to their 1982 heavy-duty truck lineup. These changes included some trim updates inside and outside of these trucks. They also made some changes on their diesel engines, which they claimed made these engines more economical than similar engines used previously. Whether these claims were true or not are hard to say since we all know that different drivers and different environments, as well as different situations, can affect fuel economy numbers.

Once again the LTL-9000 and CLT-9000 were Ford's "King of the Road" trucks. These were showboat trucks when equipped with Owner/ Operator accents and Hi-Level Custom Interior Options. And if these trucks didn't turn heads the way they were equipped from the factory Ford offered all sorts of optional extra cost accessories to really jazz them up. So much so that some of these trucks rolling down the highways looked like mobile billboards. Ford also offered dress up accessories for lesser models. When loaded up with Ford's accessories, especially bright-plated parts, Ford's plain-jane models looked like Hollywood starlets.

1983-1985

From 1983 through 1985 the major changes in Ford trucks concerned the addition of a few new tandem axle F Series trucks that, when equipped with the highest-rated springs and axles as well as heavier rated frames, could have GCWRs and GVWRs that dropped them into the heavy-duty range. By doing this Ford offered the buyer a heavy-duty truck at the cost of a medium-duty unit. These new models, the FT-800, FT-8000, and a FT-900 respectively, looked just as tough as their higher rated counterparts in the L Series and CL Series.

1986

In 1986 Ford started to use a term they called "Job Fitted Trucks." The way this program worked was that you went into your local Ford truck dealer and told him the type of truck you wanted and the type of job you expected it to do. Ford, in turn, designed a truck that fit your exact needs. In order to get customers to accept this new way of buying a truck, Ford sweetened the deal by offering all customers who opted to participate in this program a warranty that covered the complete cost of parts replacement and labor charges for 24 months and unlimited mileage on mid-range trucks, or 36 months or 300,000 miles (whichever comes first) on premium trucks.

Power was also important to the truck buyer in 1986 and to satisfy a growing need for more diesel engines, Ford expanded their diesel engine coverage to 26 choices. This was in addi-

The Fulton Fire Department of Fulton, Missouri, employs this multi-use 1982 Ford C cab to fight fires in its area. It has a Boardman 1000-gpm pump body, a 500-gallon tank, and a 75-foot aerial platform. *Dennis J. Maag Photo*

This sharp looking 1985 Ford L-9000 from the Mehlville Fire Protection District of St. Louis County, Missouri, features a 1986 Towers pump body and a Marmon-Herrington All-Wheel Drive conversion. *Dennis J. Maag Photo*

86

tion to their gasoline engine lineup for those who still preferred gas engines.

About this time Ford decided to reclassify their truck lineups by weight and size categories rather than just by GVWR and GCWR as they had done in the past. Now they had trucks in Class 6, Class 7, and Class 8 variations. Ford didn't come up with this system on their own—

by 1986 this system was being used by most truck manufacturers all across the board.

Always on the lookout to give the customer a better deal on his truck, Ford started offering additional savings on heavy-duty trucks if a customer would purchase a pre-built, pre-priced truck from Ford's Supply Center located on the grounds of Ford's Kentucky Truck Plant

Judging by how high the cab is sitting on this L Series Ford truck, it has been modified with a four-wheel drive system.

A lineup of Hadley Auto Transport L Series trucks sit in a railroad yard in Phoenix, Arizona, waiting for a new shipment of Fords to arrive.

in Louisville. This center carried a wide range of pre-assembled trucks that covered a wide range of applications. If ordering one of these trucks, Ford threw in an extended warranty that covered parts and labor for a 24- or 36-month period at no extra charge. By establishing this Truck Supply Center and pre-assembly spec vehicles Ford could keep the Kentucky Truck Plant busy during times of a downturn in the economy. If a buyer wanted to custom build a truck, or trucks, to their own specifications, that option was still open as well.

Another change of note in the 1986 model year involved Ford offering two new aftercooler systems on their CL and CLT diesel engine trucks. These systems boosted the power output as well as increased the fuel economy on trucks equipped as such. One system was designed to be used on the Cummins Formula 300 Big Cam IV engine while the other was designed specifically for the Detroit Diesel 6V-92 engine.

Prior to the mid-1980s Ford's CL-9000 and CLT-9000 trucks were designed and built for line hauling semi tractor trailer duties exclusively. However, in order to expand the truck's reach, Ford started to promote these trucks under Special Order Option Systems. These trucks also used platform bodies, box-type bodies, gasoline tanker bodies, and wrecker bodies.

Still speaking about Ford's CL Series, Ford made these trucks even more appealing by expanding their options list to include even more equipment. New items on this option list included a digital clock, an exterior-mounted sun visor, speed control, tire chain hooks, chrome-plated bumpers, driving lights, Jacobs engine brake, stainless steel quarter fenders, fuel heater, aluminum fuel tanks, instrumentation package, and a Convenience Package that included a right hand sight mirror mounted by the right hand observation window, power right hand window, and a rear cab-mounted hookup light.

This Ford L Series ten-wheel dump truck has had its grille cut away and front bumper removed to facilitate the installation of a snow plow frame.

Ford also improved their Louisville Line of trucks in this year with more equipment, more features, and new models to boot. Once again Ford's LTL-9000 was the flagship of the L Series Line, but a new variant of this model was added to the lineup. This new truck was called the "LL-9000" and it came equipped with all the "LTL-9000" features. The only difference between the two was that the LL-9000 had a single rear axle rather than the tandem rear axle setup on the LTL-9000. Like the LTL-9000, this truck was made for pulling a trailer across the country from coast to coast and everywhere in between.

Good fuel economy standards were still a top priority for most truck buyers in 1986 and Ford made sure their trucks could put up some decent numbers on the board by offering items

Here is a perfect example of a truck being used as a "rolling billboard". A deluxe version of a CLT-9000 rig it has been dressed up with a lot of bright polished aluminum trim.

Do you like Frito Lay corn chips? Well here is a trailer full of them being pulled by a CLT-9000 Ford tractor.

Notice anything different about this L-9000 Series Ford truck? It has been fitted with an "LTS-9000" front end.

This detailed shot of the side of a Louisville cab shows the tilting hood latch, Ford 9000 emblem, Custom Cab plaque mirrors, windshield trim, and assist bar.

that could enhance this cause. Items like an Aerodynamic Improvement Package, fan clutches on their engines to cut down on power loss, steel belted radial tires, overdrive transmissions, and lots of lightweight aluminum components.

This about covers all the news having to do with heavy-duty Ford trucks in 1986, but before we move onto the next chapter we should take a few moments to discuss a new Ford Tilt Cab truck that was introduced to the USA market for this year. Ford called this truck a new "C" model that fit into their medium-duty lineup in late 1985 as a new 1986 truck. The truck's official name was the "Cargo" and it was called a low tilt cab model while Ford's other "C" Tilt Cabs were called medium and high Tilt Cab models.

The Cargo was a tilt cab truck that featured European-type styling cues. This new model line consisted of about 100 models that were all powered by Ford diesel engines. As we said, this was a low Tilt Cab model that was meant to compete with other similar vehicles in the USA market by other manufacturers. Though Ford didn't say it, many in the trucking industry looked at the Cargo as a replacement for Ford's "C-Line" Tilt Cab models. Be that as it may, with the Cargo, C-Line, and CL-9000 models, Ford had the Tilt Cab market pretty well covered now from the low end all the way through to the high end.

This heavy-duty L-9000 tandem axle Ford truck carries a heavy load of oxygen tanks on a daily basis. It looks like this truck hasn't been washed in ages.

A LTL-9000 Ford tractor sits on a used car lot in Farmington, New Mexico, after unloading a shipment of used cars fresh from the auction house.

A reconditioned L-8000 tandem axle dump truck sits
on a used truck lot in Minneapolis awaiting a new
owner so it can get back to work.

1987-1989
Lowering Costs and a New Aero Look

1987

In the late 1980s Ford was looking to improve their heavy-duty truck line by adding more powerful engines to their mix of engine choices while at the same time trying to make their trucks more efficient so the costs of running them would be lower.

As far as more powerful engines go in Ford's top-of-the-line L-9000 trucks, Ford was pushing improved Cummins and Caterpillar engines for this year. Cummins's big news was their "Big Cam IV" engines that were offered up to a maximum 400 horsepower rating. Cummins was able to reach this power goal with a system they called "Optimized Aftercooling," which in layman's terms meant that they introduced a cooler charge into the engine's combustion process. Lowering the temperature of air being inducted into the engine, a denser, more oxygen-enriched mixture burns more efficiently, gives more power, and also puts cleaner emissions out of the exhaust pipe.

Caterpillar's connection to the Ford 9000 trucks in 1987 was through their 3406B engines. These engines put out power levels similar to the Cummins' engines. Like Cummins, Caterpillar also offered a power boosting aftercooler system that they called their "Jacket Water Aftercooling System." The end result was similar to the Cummins' performance. More power, more economy, and cleaner emissions.

In the 8000 Series of Ford trucks Ford also offered more powerful diesel engines from Cummins and Caterpillar. Ford also pushed their own, more powerful, diesel engines as a lower cost alternative. These Ford engines were just as tough as the Cummins and Caterpillar offerings and put out similar power ratings and fuel economy numbers of some of the other, higher priced engines. Their advantage of course was they cost less than the others. However, to some buyers the Caterpillar and Cummins names carried a lot of weight, which is why Ford offered these engines in the first place. They didn't want to lose a sale because of not having the engine a customer wanted.

Engines weren't the only items to see changes on the new 1987 Ford trucks. New rectangular halogen headlamps were featured on all 1987 L Series trucks except for the swept back axle versions. A new grille design that consisted of a series of horizontal bars was also featured on some L Series trucks in 1987. A new instrument panel was used in some of these trucks as well. Also, if you wanted a cab with a sleeper compartment that was aerodynamically de-signed, Ford had one for you. This sleeper unit was called Ford's "Aero Bullet." The unit was over seven feet tall and allowed for a driver to stand up in it if he wanted to do so.

Ford called their 1987 truck line an "Investment In Value" and they continued that theme into the 1988 model year. It could be argued that Ford added extra value into these 1988 trucks to make them even better investments.

A Ford L-8000 tractor and gasoline tanker trailer unload some fuel at an Albuquerque area gas station during the late 1980s. This one has a bug catcher mounted atop the grille surround and an electric plug poking out from under the grille.

This L-8000 Ford delivery truck spends a lot of time in cold areas as evidenced by its Ford logo canvas cover that is attached to the grille.

1988

The biggest change for 1988 involved Ford's use of more galvanized steel in their cab construction to make them more rust resistant. They didn't stop at just using a different type of steel to reach this goal. No, they spent 24 million dollars to improve the painting process at the Kentucky Truck Plant. This new, improved system included immersing the completed cab into a new priming material that was thicker, smoother, and better at oozing into all the nooks and crannies located inside and outside of the cab to better protect the base metal. The primered cabs were then subjected to a high voltage electrical charge, which helped to bond the primer to the metal better. Then the cabs were treated to some special sealers and other special coatings that were applied to critical areas that were prone to attract rust and corrosion. After all this was done the cabs were painted in a complimentary exterior color, or colors, and then that paint was allowed to dry and cure in a baking oven. Ford was so confident in this new system of painting their cabs

Here is one of the few CLT-9000 Ford trucks that we have ever seen with a van type body. A sign on the side of the truck shows that it might be carrying hazardous materials.

This battered and bruised Ford F Series heavy-duty truck still works every day hauling roofing materials to job sites and trash to the dump.

they warranted the cab for a full 60 months against corrosion. That might explain why there are still a lot of these trucks in service with cabs that don't seem to rust out.

Ford offered a few new models in 1988 to increase their market coverage. One of these new models was called an LN-7000, which gave Ford the chance to offer a lighter-duty version of a heavy-duty truck to a medium-duty truck buyer. That was a clever move on Ford's part because it gave the buyer a sense that he was getting more bang for his buck. A heavy-duty truck at a medium-duty truck price was quite a deal in anybody's book.

A couple of other new models were introduced in the Cargo line for this year as well. These new models were referred to as the CF-8000 and CFT-8000 trucks. These new heavy-duty versions of Ford's medium-duty Cargo Series replaced the C-800 models previously offered in Ford's regular "C-Line" Tilt Cab Series.

The Cargo CF-8000 and CFT-8000 ("T" stands for tandem rear axle) were powered by the same Ford diesel engines found in Ford's F, L, and C Series of trucks.

These new models were good for Ford in 1988 because they allowed them to expand their lineup to better serve a widening truck market and to offer more choices to their customers. Though the new models were good they weren't the biggest news to come out of the Ford Truck Division that year. That honor belonged to a new Ford truck that debuted at the Kentucky Truck Plant. It was a new Class 8 truck that Ford called their "Aeromax." Ford's answer to how to build the world's most advanced, aerodynamically designed conventional truck to ever hit the market, at least up until that time. Ford's goal was to create a truck that was more fuel-

Opposite page top. Another lineup of L Series Ford dump trucks that look like they have been retired from highway department road crews.

Opposite page bottom. Ford lost a pretty big customer in Hadley Auto Transport when they pulled out of the heavy-duty market segment in the late-1990s. This group of 5 or so Hadley trucks were sitting in a railroad yard waiting for some new cars to haul away.

This page top. This reconditioned L Series Ford dump truck is equipped with Ford's optional butterfly style opening hood rather than the standard tilt opening front end.

This page middle. Check out those huge flotation tires on this agricultural Ford L Series truck we found in Kansas a few years ago. Note also its special body and unique air cleaner mounted to the side of its hood.

This page bottom. Looking for a good way to haul an antique truck around? Sterling Transit has found a perfect way to do so by using one of their sharp looking Louisville tractors.

efficient. The way Ford decided to achieve this goal was to smooth out all exterior surfaces of a truck so that it could go through the air more smoothly—in other words, to cut down on power-robbing drag, and by doing so increase fuel economy numbers. Why, even the name said it all. "Aeromax" said in plain terms, "aerodynamic to the maximum."

These trucks featured set back front axles, which allowed the front fenders to be tapered back, giving the front end a smaller frontal area to penetrate the air better than say a regular Louisville truck. Along with the set back front axle and tapered set back front fenders, these trucks were also equipped with an air dam type front end, which wrapped around allowing for air to work around the front end and down the sides of the cab. Another feature found on the front end of these trucks were their aerodynamically designed wraparound rectangular halogen headlamps. These also helped to smooth out the passage of air around the front end of these trucks. Another "aero" feature added to these trucks was the front fender spats that Ford used to keep air from flowing into and out of the wheelwells. On the backside of these front fenders Ford added a set of rectangular fuel tanks and by doing so they made for a better weight distribution and these tanks could also be used as a step to get into the cab. A cab valance panel and skirts on the tanks also help

the air to move more smoothly across these services. Ford even went so far as to redesign the West Coast mirrors and turn signals to make them more aerodynamic—anything to drop down the coefficient of drag numbers on this cab design. To finish off this Aeromax truck Ford specified that a special Michelin low-resistance radial tire be used on these trucks. Though we haven't seen any information to say so, we think this truck spent a lot of time in the wind tunnel making sure that it achieved its goal of being one of the slickest trucks on the road in the late-1980s. These Aeromax trucks were the sleekest Ford trucks in the lineup that year and when equipped with Ford's "Aero Bullet" sleeper units, they were at the head of the Class 8 truck group of that year.

With all the changes we have covered in this chapter so far, one would think that Ford couldn't do any more for their truck customers in 1988. But you would be wrong because they offered even more changes to make their trucks more appealing.

In order to make their cabs look more inviting Ford redesigned their "Hi-Level" deluxe interior options for this year. They started out by reshaping their seat cushions to be more comfortable and they covered them in a new polyknit fabric that looked more plush than what was used before. That polyknit fabric was also added to the upper door trim panels and

Need to haul some dirt somewhere? This matched set of Louisville Fords can handle the job. We found them at a road project on Cape Cod in Massachusetts last year.

Opposite page bottom. The Santa Fe and Burlington Northern Railway operates this heavy-duty Ford tandem axle service truck in the Trinidad, Colorado, area. Notice the train wheels and carriage on the front of the truck allowing it to be driven on the rails.

Photo at right. Boyer Ford Trucks of Minneapolis/St. Paul, Minnesota, is one of the largest Ford dealers in the Midwest. This shop truck has been upgraded with a set of Sterling mudflaps.

headliner. The same fabric was also used to cover the mattress, curtains, panel trim, and bunk in the sleeper compartment.

In 1988 Ford also redesigned their air brake systems on most of their trucks by replacing Rockwell units and parts with Bendix units and parts.

If one needed a cut-off front bumper on a large truck, Ford offered just such an item as a Regular Production Option (RPO) on all L-8000/ 9000 trucks, LL-8000/9000 trucks, CL-9000, and CLT-9000 models. This bumper was painted in an argent silver color for most applications. Speaking of optional front bumpers, an aerodynamically designed bumper was also offered as an option on CL-9000 and CLT-9000 trucks. This bumper was usually a painted steel unit, but if a buyer wanted, it could be had in an anodized aluminum finish for an extra cost.

1988 also saw Ford expand their exterior color palette of paints for trucks. These changes included three new single solid colors, six new clear-coat deluxe colors, and a few new multi-tone combinations.

Most of Ford's diesel engine offerings were modified for this year in order to comply with new federal government standards for noise and emissions that went into effect on January 1, 1988. These engines in this modified form produced more power, had more torque on tap, and were cleaner running to boot. Ford also offered a wider range of transmissions to better cope with the power changes mandated by these new laws.

A smaller item of news affecting the world of Ford trucks this 1988 model year was the retirement of my father, Paul G. McLaughlin, from the business. After selling Ford cars and trucks for 34 years he decided that the time had come to leave the business that he so dearly loved. And the business, at least at the dealership where he worked, was definitely at a loss.

Below. A loaded LTL-9000 sits in a parking lot at a motel during an overnight stay in Albuquerque. Check out all the neat accessories on this truck.

1989

After all the changes we saw in the 1988 model year, the 1989 model year changes at Ford were minor ones at best. One big change in Ford's Class 8 trucks for this year was the availability of a Caterpillar ATAAC Series of engines that were designed to give maximum power outputs at relatively low operating speeds. For example, the CAT 3306B engine, an inline turbocharged six cylinder with a displacement of 638 cubic inches, was rated at between 285 and 300 horsepower with a gross torque rating of 1050 lbs/ft at 1350 rpm.

Or, if you needed more power, you could opt for the CAT 3406B engine that had an 893-cubic-inch displacement. This "bad boy" put out 400 horses at the same rpm level as the other Cat engine. By the way, the "ATAAC" label stood for "air to air after cooling" system. This engine was offered as an option in all Ford 9000 Series trucks of this model year.

Above. This close up front end shot shows off all the unique items found on the LTL-9000 Ford truck. A large, square looking front grille with bright-plated grille surround, dual headlights, hood side vents, and bright-plated West Coast mirrors.

Below. Here is a truck that garnered a lot of attention in 1989. This LTL-9000 Ford tractor pulled a special "25ᵗʰ Anniversary Mustang" trailer to car shows around the USA.

Close up view of the front end treatments of the new
Ford and Sterling. They both look the same, right?

1990-1998
A New Look and Time to Say Goodbye

1990

Ford came into the 1990s with a new promotional campaign to market their trucks. Ford called these trucks their "Workforce Trucks." These trucks were designed to be versatile enough to cover a wide range of job requirements. There wasn't much to talk about at the beginning of the model year as far as heavy-duty trucks are concerned, but towards the end of the 1990 model year Ford made an announcement of major proportions. After 33 continuous years of production Ford was phasing out production of their popular C Line of Tilt Cab trucks at the end of this model year.

It was rather a strange announcement since Ford ruled this market segment and had for quite sometime. Since 1957, the first year they were available, the Tilt Cab Ford had been the most popular truck of its kind. Ford's C Line Tilt Cab was the original in this class that saw quite a few competitors over the years. Most of those competitive makes stayed around for a few years before it was decided that they couldn't compete successfully against this Ford. None of them ever sold as many trucks in this market as Ford did, even in their best years.

These C Series Fords were the number one choice for buyers in certain vocational fields. Especially in the refuse, fire fighting, and city delivery businesses. Buyers in these fields liked the Tilt Cab Fords because they were roomy inside, rugged outside, had a nice styling to them, and were easy to maneuver in tight traffic conditions found in big cities.

Many in the truck business didn't think pulling the plug on these models was a smart decision on Ford's part since the truck was giving them a good return on their investment dollar. However, Ford didn't consider this move to be an unwise decision, because stopping production of this truck freed up some much needed assembly line space that they could better utilize building other types of trucks. As a matter of fact, when the decision was made to halt production of the Tilt

Cab C Series Ford, Ford already had another C model in the wings to be built at the Kentucky Truck Plant. That model line was called the Cargo, a low Tilt Cab model that Ford introduced to the USA market back in 1986. Prior to moving Cargo production to Louisville, Ford built this truck exclusively at their Iparanga, Brazil plant. Those trucks slated to come to the USA were imported by Ford, and by moving production to Louisville, Ford could save substantial costs (thus increasing the profit margins on these trucks). Moving the truck to the larger

Louisville facility, Ford could also increase production of these trucks (also helping to boost profit margins). As a matter of fact, word around the trucking business was that Ford had planned for the Cargo to replace the C Line Tilt Cabs practically from the first day these trucks landed at a port in this country. However, judging by how many C Line Tilt Cabs are still in service and how few Cargo trucks are seen in use today, there are many trucking people who think the Cargo will never replace the original C Series Tilt Cabs.

This Ford L-8000 diesel plate sits on the side of a butterfly-style opening hood. We can tell that by noting the hood opening lines and the grab handles used to secure the hood.

Three quarter rear view of a reconditioned L Series dump truck that we found on a used truck lot. It looks pretty sharp, doesn't it?

Above. This chrome yellow L-8000 tandem axle dump truck, with plow attached, sits waiting for the snow to fall again so it can get back to work.

Below. Note how the front bumper on this L-8000 trash compacting truck wraps around its front end. It does that because its front axle has been set back.

1991

The big news at Ford in 1991 had to do with Ford's release of a new, restyled AeroMax 120 model. With the AeroMax 120, Ford claimed that this truck was the most aerodynamically designed truck they ever produced, and it was easy to see why. It was one slick-looking truck from the tip of its front bumper to the rearmost part of its frame rails. It was designed from day one to manage airflow around, under, and over these new tractors.

Starting at the front of these AeroMax trucks one could see a sloping, tilting fiberglass nose that helped to smooth out the airflow coming up, around, and over the hood and front fenders. The air coming over the hood surface was directed around the wraparound windshield and then down the sides of the cab where it joined up with air coming around the fenders and fuel tanks. Flanking the nose of these trucks were a set of sculpted fenders that used flush-mounted headlamps and turn signal lamps that were designed to move air easier around them. That airflow then was directed back towards the aft end of the cab. The wraparound front bumper also moved air in a more efficient manner around the front of the cab, around the front fenders, and also back towards the rear of the cab.

Airflow down the sides of the cab was also improved by a set of fairings that were mounted behind the front tires and ran all the way back

Do you like to eat French fries? Chances are those French fries came from potatoes carried in heavy-duty L Series Ford trucks in the San Luis Valley area of Colorado.

The city of Albuquerque, New Mexico, uses this heavy-duty L Series Ford to help clean out their storm sewer systems. This truck definitely carries a lot of weight, a true tough Ford truck.

to a position in front of the rear tires. These fairing panels covered the fuel tanks and exposed parts of the frame and suspension pieces to keep air drag to a minimum.

It takes power, and lots of it, to move large heavy masses and to power these trucks Ford chose high torque, electronically controlled diesel engines from Caterpillar, Detroit Diesel, and Cummins. They then mated these engines with all sorts of transmissions and rear ends to put all that pulling power to the ground.

The AeroMax 120 was offered in day cabs or sleeper cab versions. The sleeper cab versions were available in an aero wedge shape that Ford called an "Aero Bullet." These "Aero Bullets" were available in a 42- or 60-inch depth. If you didn't really want an "Aero Bullet" wedge shape, Ford offered flat top models in 34-, 42-, or 60-inch depths. Or, if you wanted a window in your sleeper unit, Ford offered Penthouse models in 42- or 60-inch depths. If you didn't want or need a sleeper unit on the back of your cab, but still wanted the slickest aerodynamic cab you could get, Ford sold aerodynamic packages as extra cost options that added fairings to the rear sides of the cab as well as a cab

An AeroMax L-9000 tractor pulls a car hauling trailer with a full load of cars down in Australia. Look at that heavy-duty kangaroo grille guard indicating this truck makes a few trips into the Outback. *Dick Copello Collection*

A lineup of L-9000 Ford trucks sits on a used truck lot in Minneapolis, Minnesota. Judging by the large number of Ford trucks we saw in the Minneapolis area, this is definitely Ford truck country.

rooftop fairing. These fairings were made of rugged fiberglass or plastic composites that were light in weight but strong enough to handle whatever "Mother Nature" threw at them.

The AeroMax 120 was available in single or tandem rear axle configurations. The single rear axle models were designated as the LLA-9000, while the tandem rear axle type was designated as the LTLA-9000.

With the demise of the Ford C Tilt Cab models, Ford had some extra assembly room at the Kentucky Truck Plant and that extra room was taken up by Cargo truck production in the 1991 model year. Cargo production for the Latin American market was still handled at Ford's Iparanga, Brazil facility.

At the end of 1990, the Tilt Cab C Fords ceased to be and at the end of the 1991 model year Ford's CL-9000 and CLT-9000 models followed suit. Ford evidently decided that this end of the truck market wasn't that important anymore so they quietly pulled the plug on these high Tilt Cab trucks. Now, if you wanted a tilt cab Ford truck you only had the Cargo Series

Below. Ford quit producing the CL and CLT-9000 models at the end of the 1991 model year. This particular example of one is probably one of the last units built since it was bought in late 1991.

to choose from. It is really a shame that Ford decided to take these "C" and "CL" trucks out of their truck lineups because while they were available they added a little more class to the whole Ford truck line. With their demise, a void was certainly felt at the Ford truck works and with Ford truck fans worldwide.

1992

Following their successful introduction of the AeroMax 120, Ford decided to expand the AeroMax line with two new AeroMax models, the AeroMax 106 and an AeroMax 8000. In single rear axle models the AeroMax 8000 was designated as the LA-8000 while the AeroMax 106 was designated the LA-9000. In tandem

Opposite page top. An AeroMax 8000 sits beside an old F Series Ford truck. Note how Ford truck design evolved over the 20 years that separate these two vehicles.

Opposite page bottom. A pair of AeroMax 120s sitting on a used truck lot awaiting some new owners. This photo shows their sleeper units and aerodynamic fairings as well.

axle form the AeroMax 106 was designated as the LTA-9000. There was no tandem axle AeroMax 8000 model. By the way, the 106 in the AeroMax 106 stood for its BBC dimensional length of 106.3 inches while the AeroMax 120 used a longer hood to give it a BBC of 120 inches. Like its bigger "120" counterpart, the AeroMax 106 and AeroMax 8000 used set back front axles, aerodynamic front fenders, sloping hoods, etc. They were available in day cab or sleeper cab versions. Engines offered were diesel units from Cummins, Caterpillar, and Detroit Diesel.

If you didn't want, or need, an aerodynamic L Series Ford truck, Ford still offered a wide variety of conventional trucks with regular front ends as well.

1993/1994

As far as Ford trucks went, 1993 and 1994 were more of the same as what was offered in 1992. However, something happened in late 1994 that would have a profound affect on Ford's future truck offerings. That is when Ford decided to open their new Ford Commercial Truck Vehicle Center in Dearborn, Michigan.

Its creation was a part of the new "Ford 2000" master plan to streamline the company to better position it for more profitability in the future. This program of moving this center to Dearborn brought a number of responsibilities under one roof so to speak. Responsibilities that included designing, engineering, and marketing for commercial vehicles on a worldwide

A Ford L-9000 dump truck with mounted plow sits on display at a truck show in Albuquerque, New Mexico, in 1992. It is a sharp looking rig for sure.

basis would be in a centralized location now, cutting the time and developing costs for all of Ford's commercial lines. This center brought together some of the smartest and most creative of Ford's employees from all corners of the globe to work on all sorts of projects. These projects covered all Ford trucks of all sizes and shapes for the North American, Latin American, European, and Asian Pacific markets.

Another big project that had its start in 1994 was the initial pre-production at Ford's Kentucky Truck Plant of a totally redesigned series of trucks that were being prepared for the 1996 and 1997 model years.

These pre-production trial models were of Ford's new AeroMax 9500 and Louisville Line of trucks. These new models were built beside regular versions of 1994 and 1995 Ford trucks. These trucks were assembled to work out any bugs that might develop during regular production runs. They were also put together to make sure that all their parts fit together well

because Ford wanted this new truck to have a reputation for a quality built product right from the start. Some of these prototype trucks were assigned to be field tested in customer fleets on a daily basis to give Ford some valuable feedback as to how these trucks would perform in real world situations.

1995/1996

A new Ford truck was on the horizon and in July of 1995 it made its debut as a new-for-1996 model. This redesigned truck line was called the AeroMax 9500, and it had the distinction of being the first totally redesigned truck in Ford's Louisville Line since the series made its debut back in 1969.

Ford started out with a clean sheet of paper with this truck. It was a truck that would be designed from the inside out; in other words, parameters were set down for the dimensions of the cab interior and then a truck was built up around it. Most of those cab parameters were set from information supplied to Ford from

Dick Copello, who just wrote a book on car hauling vehicles, has one of his own. This photo shows his 1994 AeroMax 9000 rig that hauls cars in the Pennsylvania area. *Dick Copello Collection*

extensive surveys that were conducted with thousands of drivers and fleet operators around the country. Ford went through all this trouble so they could design a cab environment that would comfortably work out for the widest range of truck drivers they could find. The end result was a cab that was state-of-the-art, incorporating all the best ergonomic advances that had come along during the last 25 years or so.

Ford used their battery of high tech computers to create complex electronic models that showed how these cabs would react to a wide range of situations and by working with these models Ford was able to eliminate quite a few flaws before they started production. What Ford wanted to accomplish with these new cabs was to make them more comfortable, roomier, quieter, less harsh and more vibration free than

the cabs they were destined to replace. The end result was that Ford hit all those targeted goals with room to spare, according to drivers we have spoken to about these new Fords.

These new trucks featured a 4-inch longer cab with 2 to 4 more inches of seat travel. The cabs themselves were constructed of lightweight steel with doors made out of composites (plastic) to make them lighter. An aluminum-constructed cab would be offered as an option later in this truck's production cycle.

Other cab/driver oriented features included a wraparound instrument panel, 18- or 21-inch diameter steering wheels for decreasing steering effort, relocated pedals, and a relocated shifter. All were meant to cut down on the work required to operate these trucks. To make the driver more efficient was Ford's chief goal in

A lineup of new versus old Fords. Here we see an LTL-9000, a Louisville Line, L Series, and an F Series Ford.

making these changes to their cabs. These cabs also featured lighter weight doors that were 20% larger than the doors used on the old style Louisville trucks, making entry and egress from these cabs a lot easier. The cabs were also fitted with solar tinted glass that cut down on glare and ultraviolet rays coming into the cabs, making it easier for the driver and passenger to see out of the cabs (especially when they are driving towards the sun).

These new cabs were offered in day cabs or sleeper cabs, whichever the buyer wanted. The sleeper units were spacious and comfortable and were made out of aluminum with composite roof panels. For those who suffered from dust or allergies, Ford offered a new Environmental Filter Package Option that was designed to filter out dirt, dust, and pollens from the inside of the cab—a first for any truck manufacturer as far as we know. These new trucks also featured an advanced climate control system

In 1995 Ford released a redesigned 1996 Ford AeroMax 9500 model like the one shown here. Quite a dramatic change from the previous AeroMax models, wouldn't you say?

A heavy-duty B Series Ford school bus with a Bluebird body sits on the back lot of a Ford dealership in the Midwest.

to keep the entire cab area more comfortable for driver and passenger alike.

On these trucks, Ford just didn't create a new cab without taking into consideration the other aspects that make for a good truck. Looking from the front of the cab forward, these trucks featured a sloping hood line and front fender combination that helped its aerodynamic qualities. This front end was made of fiberglass and was designed to tilt forward to provide easy access to the engine and other mechanical systems. If a non-tilting front end was required, Ford offered one as an option.

A new front end design featured a new, wider, segmented grille with air intakes that flanked the grille area. Those air intakes, when combined with air extractor vents located on the sides of the hood, brought cool air into the engine compartment while heated air was drawn out. The grille was also flanked by aerodynamic headlights mounted in aerodynamically-designed front fenders that helped to direct airflow from the front of the truck around to the rear of the cab. These cabs at first had a BBC length of 113 inches, but longer cabs would

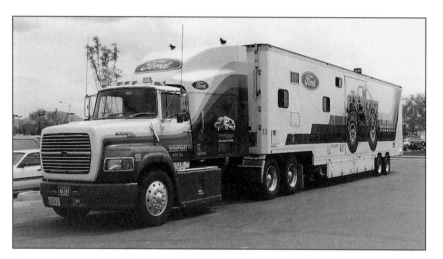

If you like monster trucks you have heard of the "Big Foot" Fords. Those "Big Foot" Fords are transported to shows around the country in these sharp looking Ford rigs.

This heavy-duty Cargo truck is being used to paint stripes on a city street in the Albuquerque, New Mexico, area in late 1999. It is loaded down with all sorts of heavy equipment.

become available later on. And finally, these cabs were placed on redesigned, lighter frames that were rated the same as similar frames on the old style L Series of trucks.

Before we talk more about Ford's new trucks, we should spend a little time talking about the changes that Ford made to their Kentucky Truck Plant to accommodate these new trucks.

The process started out with a 40-million dollar investment for new tooling for the plant. Quite a bit of that money was spent on a new robotic welding operation that would make 496 welds out of 500 used to build these new cabs. This system can weld steel or aluminum cabs to supply either to the assembly lines.

Besides the new cab building machines, the plant added a special assembly line to build these trucks concurrently with the production of the old style L Series trucks, F Series trucks, and Cargo models.

Ford also hired a number of needed employees to work at the plant to build these new trucks. Prior to the official launch or produc-

tion of these new trucks the plant celebrated a milestone event. In May of 1995 the Kentucky Truck Plant built its two-millionth vehicle since the plant opened its doors in 1969. This special truck was a white painted L Series tractor that is probably pulling a trailer cross-country these days.

The first regular production models of the new 1996 AeroMax 9500 and Louisville Line rolled off the KTP assembly lines on December 18, 1995. As mentioned before, these trucks were built alongside the old style L Series Ford trucks and would continue to be as long as the old trucks were produced. In 1995, Ford truck officials said that this dual production process would last about a year or so before the plant was completely converted over to production of the new trucks.

Trucks built in the first six months of production were referred to as Phase 1 vehicles by Ford. These new trucks were offered as Louisville Line or AeroMax 9500 trucks. The Louisville, though it shared the same cab as the

Budweiser Beer is pretty popular and so are Ford L-9000 trucks that pull their trailers. We have seen quite a few Budweiser-labeled Ford trucks in our travels around the country.

AeroMax, wasn't quite as aerodynamically clean as the former. The AeroMax had a hood that sloped down more at the front, had a different grille, different headlamp treatment, and a front bumper that was also different. The Louisville Line featured a grille that was more upright and a more squared-off look. The hood line on the Louisville also looked higher than the AeroMax. Both trucks could be had as Class 7 and Class 8 trucks and both featured BBC dimensional lengths of 113 inches.

Phase II production of these trucks began in the summer of 1996. A new 122-inch BBC AeroMax cab was added to the 113-inch BBC cab offered during the truck's first production phase. Another new feature found on some of these trucks was an aluminum cab option for those concerned with vehicle weight.

During Phase II Ford also offered the option of an integrated sleeper unit in 57- or 77-inch lengths. In the Louisville Line ranks, a new, shorter 100-inch BBC length cab with a set forward front axle was offered. A 122-inch BBC cab was also offered as an option along with the 113-inch BBC cab offered previously. All these trucks used the same cabs; they just used different hoods, front ends, fenders, and frames to achieve their different BBC lengths.

These new Ford trucks were well received and things looked pretty rosy for Ford's future in the heavy-duty truck world. So, Ford's announcement that they were selling off their heavy-duty truck interests to Freightliner in 1996 caught the trucking world by surprise. Freightliner was one of Ford's biggest Class 8 competitors and this company is part of the Daimler-Benz conglomerate. Ford, at the time they made this announcement, was sitting in second or third place on the sales list for heavy-duty trucks, so most people found it hard to understand why they were following this route.

The main reason for choosing this course of action, according to the Ford Motor Company, had to do with making profits. The light-duty truck market, especially in sports utility vehicles, was very hot at the time and Ford was making more profits on them on a per unit basis than they were making on their heavy-duty trucks and they naturally wanted to put more effort into this end of the market. By selling off the heavy-duty end they would be better suited to do that.

Ford trucks don't get much slicker looking than this AeroMax 9000 cab fitted with Ford's optional "Aero Kit."

Red, white, and blue, stars and stripes forever. This new AeroMax 9500 tractor is a hard one to miss.

Side profile shot of this CWX tractor shows that it is equipped with a set back front axle. Also note that it has been equipped with an "aero" kit.

Here is a close up shot of an AeroMax 9000 tractor. Note the full wraparound bumper and its set back front axle.

1997/1998

Ford's master plan for pulling out of this end of the market was to take a year or two. And when the process was completed, trucks that were once called Fords would become Sterlings.

With the coming of the Sterling in 1998, Ford's heavy-duty truck history came to an end—something us heavy-duty Ford truck fans thought we would never see.

Here is a close up shot of a custom Ford Motorsport AeroMax 9500 taken in 1997. Check out that extra long sleeper unit.

The look of the heaviest-duty Ford truck made today. A Super-Duty F-750 model.

MORE TITLES FROM ICONOGRAFIX:

More Great Books

NEW CAR CARRIERS 1910-1998
ISBN 1-882256-98-0

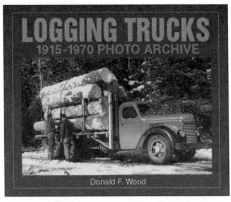

LOGGING TRUCKS 1915-1970
ISBN 1-882256-59-X

DODGE POWER WAGONS 1940-1980
ISBN 1-882256-89-1

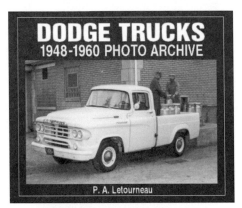

DODGE TRUCKS 1948-1960
ISBN 1-882256-37-9

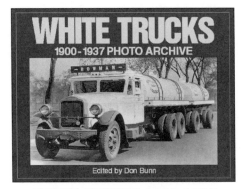

WHITE TRUCKS 1900-1937
ISBN 1-882256-80-8

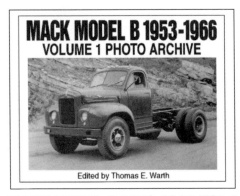

MACK MODEL B 1953-1966 VOL 1
ISBN 1-882256-19-0

All books available through:
Iconografix, Inc. PO Box 446/BK, Hudson, Wisconsin, 54016
Telephone: (715) 381-9755, (USA) (800) 289-3504, Fax: (715) 381-9756